WHAT SMALL GROUP LE
MEMBERS ARE SAYING /

EXPERIENCING CHRIST TOGETHER

My group ...
CHRIST TO...
Christ. We ...
Christ to ca...
ever.

The EXPERII...
other Bible ...
of the matte...
part.

... ...ore ...an any

...ets to the heart

...d action on my

—Leader

I love the fa...

—Member

This series i...

...nal friend.

—Leader

This series i...

...althy, maturing

small group

—Leader

EXPERIENCIN...

and how he

the living Jesus

—Member

EXPERIENCING CHRIST TOGETHER ties the heart and the mind together. The Bible knowledge grows the mind and the life application grows the heart and transforms the soul.

—Member

Other Studies in the EXPERIENCING CHRIST TOGETHER Series

Connecting in Christ Together (Fellowship)

Growing in Christ Together (Discipleship)

Serving Like Christ Together (Ministry)

Sharing Christ Together (Evangelism)

Surrendering to Christ Together (Worship)

Studies in the DOING LIFE TOGETHER Series

Beginning Life Together (God's Purpose for Your Life)

Connecting with God's Family (Fellowship)

Growing to Be Like Christ (Discipleship)

Developing Your SHAPE to Serve Others (Ministry)

Sharing Your Life Mission Every Day (Evangelism)

Surrendering Your Life to God's Pleasure (Worship)

experiencing
CHRIST
together

BEGINNING IN CHRIST TOGETHER

six sessions on
the life of Jesus

written by
BRETT and **DEE EASTMAN**
TODD and **DENISE WENDORFF**
KAREN LEE-THORP

ZONDERVAN™

GRAND RAPIDS, MICHIGAN 49530 USA

ZONDERVAN™

Beginning in Christ Together
Copyright © 2005 by Brett and Deanna Eastman, Todd and Denise Wendorff,
and Karen Lee-Thorp

Requests for information should be addressed to:
Zondervan, *Grand Rapids, Michigan 49530*

ISBN 0-310-24986-4

Interior icons by Tom Clark

Interior design by Beth Shagene & Michelle Espinoza

Printed in the United States of America

05 06 07 08 09 10 11 /❖ DCI/ 10 9 8 7 6 5 4 3 2 1

CONTENTS

Read Me First   7

SESSION 1   The Teacher   11
            Personal Health Plan   22
SESSION 2   The Healer   24
SESSION 3   The Shepherd   36
SESSION 4   The Servant   46
SESSION 5   The Savior   57
SESSION 6   The Risen Lord   73

APPENDIX
            Frequently Asked Questions   83
            LIFE TOGETHER Agreement   86
            Small Group Calendar   88
            Team Roles   89
            Personal Health Assessment   92
            Personal Health Plan   94
            Sample Personal Health Plan   96
            Journaling 101   98
            Bible Reading Plan: 30 Days   99
                through the Gospel of Mark
            Leading for the First Time   100
            Hosting an Open House   102
            EXPERIENCING CHRIST TOGETHER   103
                in a Sunday School Setting

LEADER'S NOTES   105

About the Authors   121
Small Group Roster   122

EXPERIENCING CHRIST TOGETHER

EXPERIENCING CHRIST TOGETHER: LIVING WITH PURPOSE IN COMMUNITY will take you face to face with Jesus himself. In addition to being the Son of God and Savior of the world, Jesus holds the greatest wisdom and understands the purposes for which God formed you. He knows what it takes to build authentic relationships, to know God more intensely, to grow spiritually, and ultimately to make a difference in the world. EXPERIENCING CHRIST TOGETHER offers you a chance to do what Jesus' first followers did: spend time with him, listen to what he said, watch what he did, and pattern your life after his.

Jesus lived every moment following God's purpose for his life. In this study you will experience firsthand how he did this and how you can do it too. Yet if you're anything like us, knowing what God wants for you is one thing, but doing it is something else. That's why you'll follow Jesus' plan of doing life not alone but together. As you follow in his footsteps, you'll find his pathway more exciting than anything you've imagined.

Beginning in Christ Together, the first book of this series, explores the person of Jesus Christ. Each of the subsequent five studies looks through Jesus' eyes at one of God's five biblical purposes for his people (fellowship, discipleship, service, evangelism, and worship). *Beginning in Christ Together* is about grace: what Christ has done for us. The other books are about how we live in response to grace.

Even if you've done another LIFE TOGETHER study, you'll be amazed at how Jesus can take you to places of faith you've never been before. The joy of life in him is far beyond a life you could design on your own. If you do all six study guides in this series, you'll spend one astonishing year with Jesus Christ.

Who Is Jesus?

Most people have opinions about Jesus. He was a great teacher, a revolutionary, a tragic figure caught in political intrigues, a gentle visionary, a prophet, a spiritual person with the key to enlightenment.... Or maybe he was God in some way that makes him not quite human and best kept on a respectful pedestal. Man's theories about Jesus reflect more of what people would like him to be than what the historical records of his life say about him.

But the Person who emerges from the Bible's pages is far more compelling than the theories. *Beginning in Christ Together* allows you to get to know Jesus as his first followers did. They met him as Teacher, a rabbi. They came to know him as Healer, Shepherd, Servant, Savior, and ultimately Risen Lord. From his first words, "follow me," through his ministry, death, and resurrection, he kept drawing them deeper into his life.

Jesus called his disciples to commit their lives to some challenging purposes. Those purposes weren't always easy or comfortable. What motivated Jesus' followers to do what he taught was their deep experience of who he was and what he had done for them. *Beginning in Christ Together* will ground you in that same experience so you are able to sustain your passion for Jesus' purposes over the long haul. So you can answer his call every day not because you *should* but because you *want to*, because his life burns within you. We hope your encounter with him turns your life inside out—in a good way. God has a purpose and a path for you; Jesus knows the way.

Outline of Each Session

Most people want to live a healthy, balanced spiritual life, but few achieve this by themselves. And most small groups struggle to balance all of God's purposes in their meetings. Groups tend to overemphasize one of the five purposes, perhaps fellowship or discipleship. Rarely is there a healthy balance that includes evangelism, ministry, and worship. That's why we've included all of these elements in this study so you can live a healthy, balanced spiritual life over time.

A typical group session will include the following:

 CONNECTING WITH GOD'S FAMILY (FELLOWSHIP). The foundation for spiritual growth is an intimate connection with God and his family. A few people who really know you and who earn your trust provide a place to experience the life Jesus invites you to live. This section of each session typically offers you two options. You can get to know your whole group by using the icebreaker question (always question 1), or you can check in with one or two group members— your spiritual partner(s)—for a deeper connection and encouragement in your spiritual journey.

DVD TEACHING SEGMENT. A DVD companion to this study guide is available. For each study session, a teacher discusses the topic, ordinary Christians talk about the personal experience of the topic, a scholar gives background on the Bible passage, and a leadership coach gives tips to the group leader. The DVD contains worship helps and other features as well. If you are using the DVD, you will view the teaching segment after your Connecting discussion and before your Bible study (the Growing section). At the end of each session in this study guide you will find space for your notes on the teaching segment. To view a sample of the DVD, log on to www.lifetogether.com/ExperiencingChristTogether.

GROWING TO BE LIKE CHRIST (DISCIPLESHIP). Here is where you come face to face with Christ. In a core Bible passage you'll see Jesus in action, teaching or demonstrating some aspect of how he wants you to live. The focus won't be on accumulating information but on how Jesus' words and actions relate to what you say and do. We want to help you apply the Scriptures practically, creatively, and from your heart as well as your head. At the end of the day, allowing the timeless truths from God's Word to transform our lives in Christ is our greatest aim.

FOR DEEPER STUDY. If you want to dig deeper into more Bible passages about the topic at hand, we've provided additional passages and questions. Your group may choose to do study homework ahead of each meeting in order to cover more biblical material. Or you as an individual may choose to study the For Deeper Study passages on your own. If you prefer not to do study homework, the Growing section will provide you with plenty to discuss within the group. These options allow individuals or the whole group to go deeper in their study, while still accommodating those who can't do homework or are new to your group.

You can record your discoveries on the Reflections page at the end of each session. We encourage you to read some of your insights to a friend (spiritual partner) for accountability and support. Spiritual partners may check in each week over the phone, through email, or at the beginning of the group meeting.

DEVELOPING YOUR GIFTS TO SERVE OTHERS (MINISTRY). Jesus trained his disciples to discover and develop their gifts to serve others. God has designed you uniquely to serve him in a way no other person can. This section will help you discover and use your God-given design. It will also encourage your group to discover your unique design as a community. In two sessions in this study, you'll put into practice what you've learned in the Bible study by taking a step to serve others. These simple steps will take your group on a faith journey that could change your lives forever.

 SHARING YOUR LIFE MISSION EVERY DAY (EVANGELISM). Many people skip over this aspect of the Christian life because it's scary, relationally awkward, or simply too much work for their busy schedules. But Jesus wanted all of his disciples to help outsiders connect with him, to know him personally. This doesn't mean preaching on street corners. It could mean welcoming a few newcomers into your group, hosting a short-term group in your home, participating in a cross-cultural missions project, or walking through this study with a friend. In four sessions of this study, you'll have an opportunity to take a small step in this area. These steps will take you beyond Bible study to Bible living.

 SURRENDERING YOUR LIFE FOR GOD'S PLEASURE (WORSHIP). God is most pleased by a heart that is fully his. Each group session will give you a chance to surrender your heart to God in prayer and worship. You may read a psalm together, share a page in your journal, or use one of the songs on the DVD to open or close your meeting. (Additional music is available on the LIFE TOGETHER Worship DVD/CD series, produced by Maranatha!) If you have never prayed aloud in a group before, no one will put pressure on you. Instead, you'll experience the support of others who are praying for you. This time will knit your hearts in community and help you surrender all your hurts and dreams into the hands of the One who knows you best.

STUDY NOTES. This section provides background notes on the Bible passage(s) you examine in the Growing section. You may want to refer to these notes during your group meeting or as a reference for those doing additional study.

REFLECTIONS. At the end of each session is a blank page on which you can write your insights from your personal time with God. Whether you do deeper Bible study, read through the Gospels, meditate on a few verses, or simply write out your prayers, you'll benefit from writing down what you discover. You may want to pick up a blank journal or notepad after you fill in these pages.

THE TEACHER

The novel *Across the Nightingale Floor* is a classic hero tale set in an imagined ancient Japan. Cut off by tragedy from his childhood world, Takeo sets out to forge a new life as the adopted son of Lord Shigeru. Shigeru is nothing like the villagers among whom Takeo was raised, but the teenager quickly decides he wants to be just like Shigeru when he becomes a man. It's not just that Shigeru has saved his life. Shigeru also has qualities that Takeo wants: wisdom, patience, kindness, and the skills and honor of a warrior. Takeo commits his life to emulating his adopted father/master and fulfilling Shigeru's goals.

Like Takeo, we were born to bring about significant good in the world. But who can save our lives and then show us how to live them? Jesus can. In this study, you'll meet Jesus as his first followers met him. Whether you have been committed to him for years or are checking him out for the first time, this is your chance to look at him with fresh eyes. Who is he really, and does he embody the qualities of a hero worth following?

CONNECTING WITH GOD'S FAMILY   20 min.

Just as we have all had first impressions of Jesus, so we all have first impressions of each other. Sharing pieces of our stories helps us know each other better, just as the stories about Jesus give us a clearer picture of him. In this study, you're going to connect with Christ and each other at a deeper level. To get the most out of this experience, it's worth taking some time to learn more about one another.

1. Respond to both of the following:

   Who was one of your childhood heroes? How was that person heroic to you?

What do you hope to get out of this study?

2. Whether your group is brand new or ongoing, it's always important to reflect on and review your values together. On pages 86–87 is a sample agreement with the values we've found most useful in sustaining healthy, balanced groups. We recommend that you choose one or two values—ones you haven't previously focused on or have room to grow in—to emphasize during this study. Choose ones that will take your group to the next stage of intimacy and spiritual health.

☐ *For new groups:* You may want to focus on welcoming newcomers or on sharing group "ownership." Any group will quickly move from being "the leader's group" to "our group" if everyone shares a small role. See pages 89–91 for help on how to do this well.

☐ *For existing groups:* We recommend that you rotate host homes on a regular basis and let the hosts lead the meeting. We've come to realize that healthy groups rotate leadership. This helps to develop every member's ability to shepherd a few people in a safe environment. Even Jesus gave others the opportunity to serve alongside him (Mark 6:30–44). Session 3 will explain how to set up a rotating schedule.

GROWING TO BE LIKE CHRIST   40 min.

When Simon, Andrew, James, and John first met Jesus, they were already looking for something more in their lives than just fishing (John 1:35–42). They were looking for the Messiah, a King who would free God's people from oppression and usher in God's kingdom of justice. They thought Jesus might be the one. At their first meeting, they addressed him as "Rabbi" or "Teacher" (verse 38). In those days a rabbi wasn't just an academic lecturer, and a student or "disciple" wasn't interested in mere information. A rabbi taught truth to base one's life on. Jesus wasn't someone who made his disciples think, "I want to know what he knows," but someone who made them think, "I want to be like him."

3. Have someone read aloud Mark 1:14–20. If this were all the information you had, what would you say motivated the four fishermen to leave their jobs and follow Jesus?

4. In verse 15, Jesus summarizes his entire teaching. If we deeply understand this verse, we understand the essence of his message.
   Read the study note on "the kingdom of God." How would you explain verse 15 in your own words?

5. "Repent" is a scary word for many people today. After all, it asks us to think and act differently. Why is repentance necessary if we want to experience God's kingdom? (You may want to refer to the study note on "repentance.")

6. Read Mark 1:21–39. Here Mark shows a broad picture of Jesus' early ministry. What are the various things he did?

   How did people respond?

7. What was the connection between Jesus' actions and his message?

8. Jesus' "authority" amazed people (verses 22, 27). What is authority?

9. Jesus gives us the same invitation he gave his first disciples: *Repent. Believe the good news. Follow me.* How is this different from merely believing a set of facts about Jesus and about how we get to heaven?

10. If Jesus has authority—to summon followers, to teach how to live a good life, to heal, to free people from evil spirits—what authority do you think he wants you to give him in your life today?

FOR DEEPER STUDY

Luke 5:1–11 presents an expanded version of the day when Jesus called Simon, Andrew, James, and John. John 1:35–42 presents Simon and Andrew's first encounter with Jesus, which took place days or weeks earlier. What do these add to your picture of Jesus? What qualities or actions attracted these men to Jesus?

Mark 4:1–34 records some of Jesus' teaching. What do you learn about the kingdom from these stories?

Isaiah 50:4–11 is an Old Testament portrait of a true disciple. Jesus lived this way. What features of this portrait seem most significant to you?

DEVELOPING YOUR GIFTS TO SERVE OTHERS — 20 min.

11. EXPERIENCING CHRIST TOGETHER is an opportunity to do what Jesus' first disciples did: follow him around and learn to pattern your life after his. You'll make this a priority to the degree that you're convinced that he has "authority" (Mark 1:27)—that he really is the expert on living a healthy, balanced life.

   Jesus had five basic life purposes he wanted his followers to pursue. One is what we call discipleship or "Growing to Be Like Christ." That is, living as a disciple of Christ the Teacher. Are you ready to let Jesus be your personal trainer in how to live? If so, which of the following growth steps are you willing to take on for the next six weeks?

   ☐ *Prayer.* Jesus habitually set aside time alone to pray (Mark 1:35). When can you make time for prayer each day? If you're new to prayer, you might try just five minutes a day when you get up in the morning or when you arrive at work. You could pray, "Jesus, train me to live today. Train me to think your thoughts. Train me to feel toward people what you feel. Train me to do what you would do." Then review your day with him. You may find it helpful to write your prayer in a journal or on the Reflections page (page 20).

☐ *Gospel Reading.* On page 99 is a plan for reading through the gospel of Mark in thirty days. We recommend that you jot down your thoughts on the Reflections page or in a journal.

☐ *Meditation.* If you've read Mark before, try meditation as a way of internalizing God's Word more deeply. Copy a portion of Mark 1:14–39 onto a card, and tape it somewhere in your line of sight, such as your car's dashboard or the kitchen table. Think about it when you sit at red lights, or while you're eating a meal. What is God saying to you, here and now, through these words? Several alternative passages for meditation are suggested on the Reflections page in each session.

12. Pair up with someone in your group. (We suggest that men partner with men and women with women.) This person will be your "spiritual partner" during this study. He or she doesn't have to be your best friend but will simply encourage you to complete the goal you set in question 11. Following through on a resolution is tough when you're on your own, but we've found it makes all the difference to have a partner cheering us on.

On pages 22–23 is a Personal Health Plan, a chart for keeping track of your spiritual progress. In the box that says, "WHO are you connecting with spiritually?" write your partner's name. In the box that says, "WHAT is your next step for growth?" write the step(s) you chose in question 11. You have now begun to address two of God's five purposes for your life! You can see that the health plan contains space for you to record the ups and downs of your progress each week in the column labeled "My Progress." And now with your spiritual partner you don't have to do it alone, but together with a friend.

Tell your partner what step you chose. When you check in with your partner each week, the "Partner's Progress" column on this chart will provide a place to record your partner's progress in the goal he or she chose. If you have more than one partner, an extra Personal Health Plan can be found on pages 94–95 or downloaded from www.lifetogether.com/healthplan.

On pages 96–97 you'll find a completed health plan filled in as an example. For now, don't worry about the WHERE, WHEN, and HOW questions on the health plan.

SURRENDERING YOUR LIFE FOR GOD'S PLEASURE   15–30 min.

13. Allow everyone to answer this question: "How can we pray for you this week?" Be sure to write these requests on your Prayer and Praise Report on page 19.

14. Worship comes naturally when we truly see Jesus as the King of his kingdom, our Master and Teacher, the One with authority over disease and evil. What kind of worship fits your group? Here are two ideas:

☐ Use a song from the DVD, the LIFE TOGETHER Worship DVD/CD set, or a CD of your choice, to worship God with music.

☐ Psalm 119 praises what God teaches in the Old Testament. It's equally relevant to Jesus, our Teacher. Have someone read aloud Psalm 119:33–40 to begin your worship time. You may also read the passage aloud together.

STUDY NOTES

Something about Jesus drew Simon, Andrew, James, and John. What was it? Luke and John said the four fishermen spent time with Jesus and even saw him do miracles before they decided to follow him (Luke 5:1–11; John 1:35–42). But Mark focused on Jesus' message. Jesus spoke with authority like no other rabbi they had known. And his actions backed his words.

The kingdom of God (Mark 1:15). The realm in which God's will is done God's way (Matthew 6:10), a realm of goodness, joy, and beauty. Most of the universe is part of God's kingdom because the stars and planets function exactly as God made them to function. Our planet withdrew from God's kingdom when humans (whom God had put in charge) rebelled against him. The Bible tells the story of how God has been working for millennia to bring us back into his kingdom.

God created the nation of Israel to be an outpost of his kingdom, to attract the rest of humanity to rejoin his kingdom. But Israel repeatedly failed to obey God's commands. As a result, God let one empire after another oppress them. By the time of Jesus, the Roman Empire was in charge. Many Jews were desperate for a leader who would throw out the Romans and restore God's kingdom politically and spiritually. This much-prophesied leader would be called the Messiah (Greek: Christ). Gossip swirled around every potential leader: could this be the Messiah?

Jesus was the Messiah, and God's kingdom was the central issue of his teaching. But he had no intention of being a military Messiah to oust the Romans and establish a political kingdom. Instead, he invited everyone to stop pursuing their own agendas and rejoin God's realm of justice and joy. God's kingdom was (and is) immediately available in part to anyone who would follow Jesus. But only in part. Christ will bring his kingdom in its fullness when he returns.

Repent (1:15). The Greek word here means to change your mind. To think about things in a radically different way. A related Hebrew word means to change course, to look for what you need in a completely different direction. Feeling bad about your behavior or yourself is called "remorse" and is useful only when it leads to a change in behavior. We can't always decide to change our thinking—we don't know what we don't know, so God often has to take the initiative. Our job is *humility*: the willingness for God to change our minds, the willingness to say, "I'm wrong. I'll change course. I'll do it your way."

Follow me (1:17). Believing in Jesus as an intellectual exercise wasn't enough. Jesus wanted followers—people who would be with him constantly over years so he could train them to be who God made them to be. His disciples were like apprentices who imitated everything he did.

PRAYER AND PRAISE REPORT

Briefly share your prayer requests with the large group, making notations below. Then gather in small groups of two to four to pray for each other.

Date: _____

Prayer Requests

_____
_____
_____
_____
_____
_____
_____
_____
_____
_____

Praise Report

_____
_____
_____
_____
_____
_____
_____
_____
_____
_____
_____

REFLECTIONS

Use this page to write out your prayers, your thoughts about your daily Bible reading, or your meditations on a verse from the passage you have already studied. Below are some suggested verses for meditation. The Bible Reading Plan is on page 99.

For Meditation: Mark 1:15 or 1:17

For Gospel Reading:

- What do I *learn* from the life of Christ (his identity, personality, priorities)?

- How does he want me to *live* differently?

_____

_____

_____

_____

_____

_____

_____

_____

_____

_____

_____

_____

_____

_____

_____

_____

_____

_____

_____

DVD NOTES

If you are watching the accompanying *Beginning in Christ Together* DVD, write down what you sense God is saying to you through the speaker. (If you'd like to hear a sample of the DVD teaching segment, go to www.lifetogether.com/ExperiencingChristTogether.)

PERSONAL HEALTH PLAN

This worksheet could become your single most important feature in this study. On it you can record your personal priorities before the Father. It will help you live a healthy spiritual life, balancing all five of God's purposes.

PURPOSE	PLAN
CONNECT	WHO are you connecting with spiritually?
GROW	WHAT is your next step for growth?
DEVELOP	WHERE are you serving?
SHARE	WHEN are you shepherding another in Christ?
SURRENDER	HOW are you surrendering your heart?

If you have more than one partner, another Personal Health Plan can be found in the Appendix or downloaded in a larger format at www.lifetogether.com/healthplan. A Sample Health Plan is also in the Appendix.

DATE	MY PROGRESS	PARTNER'S PROGRESS

SESSION 2 THE HEALER

Paul attended his church's annual men's retreat but was mentally checked out for most of the event. He had decided that when he got home, he was going to move out of the house. He was done with marriage.

Paul was sharing a room with members of his small group. He told them about his decision. Shocked, they recognized a chance to be Christ-in-the-flesh for Paul. After the Saturday night program, they gathered in their room and prayed for him. They prayed for what seemed like hours.

God spoke to Paul in that moment. Although his marriage seemed hopeless, his friends gave him hope that Jesus could heal it. When Paul got home, he told his wife he wanted to stay married and change some fundamental things. God began to do something new in Paul's heart and in his marriage.

In this session you're going to look at Christ as the Healer. He healed Paul's heart, and he wants to heal you today.

CONNECTING WITH GOD'S FAMILY   10 min.

As people are gathering, play a song from the LIFE TOGETHER Worship series or any worship CD. When the song ends, pray briefly for God's presence in your time together. Then get started, either with the group check-in question (question 1) or with a few minutes for spiritual partners to check in with each other (question 2).

1. As you prepare to talk about Christ as the Healer, which of the following best describes your personal health (physical, emotional, spiritual) right now?

   ☐ I'm so healthy I can leap tall buildings in a single bound.
   ☐ I'm sound as a bell, but nothing extraordinary.
   ☐ I'm surviving but not thriving.
   ☐ The pain in my neck is . . .
   ☐ I'm depending on life support.
   ☐ Call 911!

   Or,

2. Sit with your spiritual partner(s). If your partner is absent or if you are new to the group, join with another pair or with someone who is also partnerless.

Turn to your Personal Health Plan (pages 22–23). Share with your partner(s) how your time with God went this week. What is one thing you discovered? Or, what obstacles hindered you from following through? Make a note about your partner's progress and how you can pray for him or her.

GROWING TO BE LIKE CHRIST   40 min.

As in session 1, imagine yourself as one of Jesus' first disciples. You're following Jesus around—watching what he does, listening to what he says, learning what he cares about. As he talks about the kingdom—the realm where God accomplishes his purposes—Jesus is doing the works of the kingdom.

Most of those works involve healing. God cares passionately about people, so restoring what is broken in their lives is at the core of his purposes. Jesus' actions say, "These healings are the things the King wants done. They're happening now because the kingdom is here!"

3. Read Mark 1:40–45. From this scene, how would you describe Jesus' character and values?

4. In Mark 1:22, 27, people talked about Jesus' "authority"—his authority to teach what was true and even to cast out evil spirits. Read Mark 2:1–12. How does the issue of authority play out in this scene?

5. What's the connection between Jesus' authority to heal, to teach, and to forgive sins? Why would healing validate Jesus' authority in the other areas?

6. In Mark 2:7, Mark reveals one reason why the religious leaders turned against Jesus: blasphemy. Read the study note on forgiving sins on page 31. In their shoes, would you have suspected Jesus of blasphemy? Why or why not?

Why did Jesus have the authority to forgive sins against God?

7. Read Mark 2:13–17. The study note on page 31 offers some background on tax collectors. What do you learn about Jesus (his character, his priorities) from this scene?

8. Why does Jesus compare sinners with the sick in verse 17?

9. From what you have studied so far, how much importance did Jesus place on physical healing as compared to spiritual healing (the forgiveness of sins)?

10. Why do you think Jesus hung around outcasts more than the religious class?

What are the implications for you and your group?

FOR DEEPER STUDY

What was the connection between healing and God's kingdom? See Isaiah 35:5–10; 61:1–3; Luke 4:14–21; 7:18–23. What does it say about God that healing (physical, spiritual) is such an important part of his kingdom? Yet if healing is so important, why didn't Jesus heal everybody, and why doesn't God physically heal all believers now?

Healing figured in the ministry of some earlier prophets (2 Kings 4:1–37; 5:1–14). How was Jesus' healing ministry similar to, and how was it different from, that of the prophets?

What could the disciples learn about sharing the good news of the kingdom from Jesus (Mark 1:41), the leper (1:45), the friends of the paralytic (2:1–5), and Levi and Jesus (2:15–17)?

SHARING YOUR LIFE MISSION EVERY DAY   15 min.

In Mark 1:17, Jesus told his disciples he was going to teach them "how to fish for people" (NLT). That is, he was going to show them how to do evangelism or share the good news (what we call "Sharing Your Life Mission"). Evangelism is one of the five biblical purposes of the church—the things that are urgent to God. It was one of Jesus' priorities and is one of the reasons why we're here on earth.

For us, sharing our faith is a way of participating in God's kingdom. We've found that groups which include an outward focus grow much deeper in their relationships than those which look only inward.

11. Who are the people in your life who need to meet Jesus or know him more deeply? The "Circles of Life" diagram on the next page will help you think of the various people you come in contact with on a regular basis. Prayerfully write down at least three or four names in the circles.

   ☐ The beginning of a new series is a wonderful time to welcome a few friends into your group. Which of the people you listed could you invite? Like the friends of the paralytic in Mark 2, help your friend overcome obstacles to coming to a place where he or she can encounter Jesus. Does your friend need a ride to the group? Help with child care?

   ☐ Is there someone whom you wouldn't invite to your group but who still needs a connection? Would you be willing to have lunch or coffee with that person, catch up on life, and share something you've learned from this study? Jesus doesn't call all of us to lead small groups, but he does call every disciple to spiritually multiply his or her life over time.

CIRCLES OF LIFE

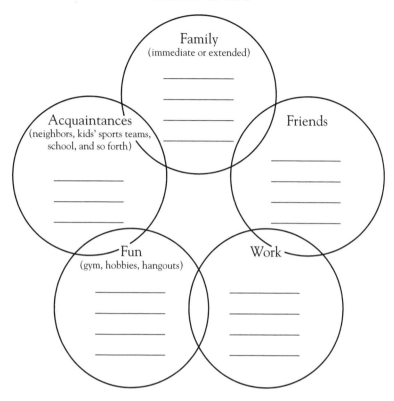

In your Personal Health Plan on page 22, next to the "Sharing" icon, answer the WHEN question: "WHEN are you shepherding another in Christ?"

12. Levi introduced his friends to Jesus at a party. He wasn't ashamed of his friends, and he wasn't ashamed of Jesus. Jesus didn't care what religious people thought because his purpose was clear: he came to call the lost, to share his life with them.

    Who are the one or two party animals in your group? Who loves to gather a few friends or family? Especially if your group is brand new, we urge you to plan a group party sometime in the next few weeks. It could be as simple or elaborate as you like. Getting to know each other should be a priority for a new group, and a party is a great help.

    And if you really want to do things the way Jesus did them, invite your friends who don't go to church. If you don't have any unchurched friends, get some! Invite those neighbors you've never gotten around to. Invite a coworker. Simply send out postcards or email invitations to your friends, family, and neighbors.

You don't have to present the whole gospel message at this party—just demonstrate the presence of God's kingdom by your love for your fellow group members and your guests. You'll have a blast.

So if you love to throw parties, why not volunteer to serve your group in this way? Who would like to make this happen?

SURRENDERING YOUR LIFE FOR GOD'S PLEASURE   20 min.

13. Christ is present in your group as the Healer and Forgiver. Gather in smaller circles of three or four people. Share with one another how you would like to experience healing or forgiveness from Christ. Be sure to have everyone write down the personal requests of the members in each circle. (The Prayer and Praise Report is on page 33.)

Then pray for one another in your circle. Don't put pressure on anyone to pray aloud. When you pray for each person, you may find it meaningful to hold hands or place your hands on another person's shoulder. Jesus often touched those he healed to communicate his care for them.

STUDY NOTES

Leprosy (Mark 1:40). This term included a wide variety of skin diseases. They were not only physical diseases (sometimes horribly painful and disfiguring) but also social diseases. Many skin diseases were contagious, and many more rendered lepers and those who touched them "unclean" for worship in the temple (Leviticus 13:45–46). Because people feared contact with them, lepers became outcasts. For a rabbi like Jesus to touch a leper was astounding.

Don't tell this to anyone (1:44). Sometimes Jesus did miracles publicly, but sometimes he healed people privately and asked them not to give him credit. He may have wanted to keep the masses from proclaiming him the Messiah until he'd had time to demonstrate what kind of Messiah he was. While they expected a military Messiah, Jesus' actual mission was to overthrow sin and death through his own death. Also, Jesus avoided crass self-promotion that would make him a mere celebrity (John 7:1–8). Instead, he carefully chose moments for public declarations (John 7:14, 37–44). His priority was preaching the good news of God's kingdom. Before healing the leper, he had been able to do this in the town synagogues throughout Galilee, but after the former leper spread the news of the miracle, Jesus was so swamped with crowds wanting miracles that his preaching ministry was hindered (Mark 1:45).

Sins (2:5). Until we reorient our lives around Christ, sin means we've missed something crucial. It's not that we tried to follow God's ways and fell short, it's that we failed altogether. Sin is disobeying God's direct commands outlined in Exodus 20:1–17 and revisited in Matthew 5:21–48. At the highest level, sin is a failure to obey the Great Commandments of loving God, loving our neighbor, and loving other Christians. At its heart, sin—like righteousness—is relational.

Who can forgive sins but God alone? (2:7). Jews didn't believe that even the Messiah would have the right to forgive sins on God's behalf. Consider how sin and forgiveness work. First, when we harm another person, we sin against that person. When we do what we want rather than what God wants, then we sin against God. Therefore, all sin is ultimately against God (in addition to any other injured parties). Second, the only person who can forgive a sin is the one who was harmed. You can't forgive your neighbor's son for crashing your neighbor's car. It's not your business. God is the owner of the planet we have crashed, so God is the only One who has the right to issue blanket forgiveness.

Tax collectors (2:15). These were Roman-employed Jews who made money by extracting taxes from their fellow Jews. The Romans required a certain total sum from a given geographic area; anything more the tax collector could get was his profit. Tactics included extortion and violence. Devout Jews understandably hated tax collectors.

Pharisees (2:16). One of the most highly regarded Jewish sects at that time, the Pharisees followed a strict interpretation of the biblical law based on centuries of tradition. Jesus shared a number of the Pharisees' interpretations, such as the need for personal holiness, the importance of loving one's neighbor, and the resurrection of the dead. However, he angered them by rejecting other interpretations (for example, healing on the Sabbath, which the Pharisees viewed as work), forgiving sins, and associating with immoral people. Also, some Pharisees were blind to the sinful condition of their own hearts and focused on other people's sin.

PRAYER AND PRAISE REPORT

Briefly share your prayer requests with the large group, making notations below. Then gather in small groups of two to four to pray for each other.

Date: _____

Prayer Requests

_____

_____

_____

_____

_____

_____

_____

_____

_____

_____

Praise Report

_____

_____

_____

_____

_____

_____

_____

_____

_____

_____

REFLECTIONS

Use this page to write out your prayers, your thoughts about your daily Bible reading, or your meditations on a verse from the passage you have already studied. Below are some suggested verses for meditation. The Bible Reading Plan is on page 99.

For Meditation: Mark 1:41–42 or 2:8–12

For Gospel Reading:

• What do I *learn* from the life of Christ (his identity, personality, priorities)?

• How does he want me to *live* differently?

DVD NOTES

If you are watching the accompanying *Beginning in Christ Together* DVD, write down what you sense God is saying to you through the speaker. (If you'd like to hear a sample of the DVD teaching segment, go to www.lifetogether.com/ExperiencingChristTogether.)

_____

_____

_____

_____

_____

_____

_____

_____

_____

_____

_____

_____

_____

_____

_____

_____

_____

_____

_____

_____

_____

_____

_____

_____

THE SHEPHERD

For Cara, college was a season of experimenting, testing, deciding what was really worth living for. Although she had put her life into the hands of Jesus Christ some years earlier, she wandered away from the Shepherd and his flock during these college years. She was drawn toward what looked like a greener pasture: seeking happiness in entertainment and fun instead of living for something greater.

But Jesus loved her. Through the people he put into Cara's life, he showed his desire to protect her from harm and feed her soul. People continually reached out to include her—in a campus Christian group, a Bible study, a Christian event. Jesus never gave up pursuing her. After many invitations, she returned to the people of God. She realized that these people and their Shepherd, rather than her party friends, genuinely cared about her.

CONNECTING WITH GOD'S FAMILY   10 min.

You've encountered Jesus as Teacher and Healer. Next you'll consider him as Shepherd. Your past experience with care and guidance (or the lack of them) will affect your relationship with Jesus the Shepherd. Sharing those past experiences is a great way to get to know each other better. Question 1 is an opportunity to do that. You may discuss it as a whole group, or if spiritual partners are meeting one on one, they can answer question 1 quickly with each other and then move on to question 2.

1. When you were growing up, how much nurture, care, and wise guidance did you receive from your family and others? Roughly rate your experience on a scale of 0 to 5.

   0   1   2   3   4   5

   I was pretty much   I got a lot of terrific
   on my own.   care and guidance.

   Or,

2. Check in with your spiritual partner(s), or with another partner if yours is absent. Share something God taught you during your time in his Word this week, or read a brief section from your journal. Be sure to write down your partner's progress on page 23.

GROWING TO BE LIKE CHRIST   40 min.

Sheep and shepherds were common sights in Jesus' day. Sheep were neither strong enough nor smart enough to survive the often harsh Middle East environment on their own. Without the constant care of a shepherd, they would die from thirst or bad water, from cold or attack by wolves, or just from falling over and having too much bulk to stand up. The Old Testament prophets spoke of the nation's citizens as sheep and the leaders as shepherds who either neglected or exploited them.

We too need the care, protection, and guidance of a Shepherd. However, if we're used to looking out for ourselves, allowing Christ to shepherd us requires a shift in the way we operate. For some of us, it's hard to let down our defenses and trust Christ to guide and care for us well.

3. Read John 10:1–10, and imagine a sheep pen with one gate. In what ways is Jesus like the gate of a sheep pen?

4. In what ways is Jesus like the shepherd in John 10:1–6?

5. Read John 10:11–18. In what additional ways is Jesus a good shepherd?

6. Jesus says he came in order that we, the sheep, "may have life, and have it to the full" (verse 10). Other translations speak of "abundant" life. What do you think a full or abundant life involves?

Are you experiencing abundant life? If so, please give a brief example. If not, what's missing for you?

7. What do you think Jesus means when he says his sheep know and listen to his voice (verses 3–4, 16)?

8. Because thieves and wolves want to steal or devour the sheep, the Good Shepherd is willing to die to rescue them (verses 11, 15, 17–18). Who or what have been the thieves or wolves in your life?

9. How are you experiencing the loving care of the Good Shepherd?

10. In what ways do you struggle with letting the Shepherd lead you to a better life?

11. Jesus' heart ached for sheep without shepherds. Why did their shepherdless state grieve him so much?

How did it move him to respond?

FOR DEEPER STUDY

How did the Old Testament prophets use the shepherds/sheep image to portray what was wrong with Israel's leaders (Isaiah 56:9–11; Jeremiah 23:1–4; Ezekiel 34:1–10)?

What did God promise to do about the problem of bad shepherds (Isaiah 40:10–11; Ezekiel 34:22–24)?

How does Jesus further use the shepherd image to explain his own mission and the Father's heart (Luke 15:1–7)?

How does Peter adapt the same image when he instructs leaders and members of the early church (1 Peter 5:1–4)?

What is most personally significant to you about the image of shepherds and sheep?

DEVELOPING YOUR GIFTS TO SERVE OTHERS 20 min.

Jesus has a vision that every sheep will find a shepherd. This is a kingdom vision—a priority that God wants done in the world. First and foremost, he wants to connect each sheep with himself, the chief Shepherd. He also invites us to train as under-shepherds, caring for a few of his sheep. Even if you're not called to pastor a large flock, you may be called to shepherd a few of God's sheep at work, in your neighborhood, or even in a small group someday. You can help to connect seekers with the Shepherd or help a new believer learn to respond to the Shepherd's voice. In some way, God has uniquely gifted you to participate in his work in the world. If you're open, God will equip you.

12. In session 2 (question 12) you had two members volunteer to plan a party—ideally with a few of your friends, neighbors, or coworkers who don't have a church or small group. This is a great way to have everybody take a huge step of faith and reach out together. We know one group that sent out invitations at the end of their first six weeks together, and over thirty-five of their neighbors joined them!

Give those volunteers a chance to update the group on the plan. What help do they need?

13. "Rotating leaders" is one of the group values we highly recommend for your group. People need opportunities to experiment

with ways in which God may have gifted them. Your group will give you all the encouragement you need before, during, and after the session.

We also suggest you rotate host homes, with the host of each meeting providing the refreshments. Some groups like to let the host lead the meeting each week, while others like to let one person host while another person leads.

The Small Group Calendar on page 88 is a tool for planning who will host and lead each meeting. Take a few minutes to plan hosts and leaders for your next three meetings. Don't pass this up! It will revolutionize your group.

SURRENDERING YOUR LIFE FOR GOD'S PLEASURE   20 min.

14. As a group read aloud Psalm 23. Then allow some open time for people to thank God for the ways he shepherds you. If praying aloud is new for you, you can simply say, "Thank you, God, for ..."

Also, pray for those in your group who especially need care from the Good Shepherd right now.

STUDY NOTES

Sheep follow him because they know his voice (John 10:4). In English-speaking countries, shepherds typically drive sheep with the help of sheepdogs. In the Holy Land, shepherds lead sheep by their voice, and the sheep follow them. It's a more personal connection. They respond to the voice of one they have grown to trust. Shepherds of Jesus' day would herd their sheep to safe pasture, providing protection along the way. Jesus is the shepherd of Psalm 23, the One who protects us from the roaring lion (1 Peter 5:8).

I have come that they may have life, and have it to the full (10:10). The word for "full" (from Greek: *perissos*) is rendered as "abundant" in other translations. It means beyond measure, over and above, more than necessary, surpassing. Life that good can come only from the One who desires to shepherd us to a better life. We often miss out on all that Jesus has for us when we fail to see him as our Shepherd and follow his lead to an abundant life.

I lay down my life—only to take it up again (10:17). Sheep were highly prized but stupid. They were protected at all cost and needed that protection. The ultimate test of a shepherd was his willingness to lay down his life for his sheep (1 Samuel 17:34–36). Jesus is that kind of Shepherd to us. He willingly laid down his life on the cross for our sake, demonstrating his sacrificial love for us.

PRAYER AND PRAISE REPORT

Briefly share your prayer requests with the large group, making notations below. Then gather in small groups of two to four to pray for each other.

Date: _____

Prayer Requests

_____

_____

_____

_____

_____

_____

_____

_____

_____

_____

Praise Report

_____

_____

_____

_____

_____

_____

_____

_____

_____

_____

_____

REFLECTIONS

Use this page to write out your prayers, your thoughts about your daily Bible reading, or your meditations on a verse from the passage you have already studied. Below are some suggested verses for meditation. The Bible Reading Plan is on page 99.

For Meditation: John 10:9–10 or 10:11

For Gospel Reading:

- What do I *learn* from the life of Christ (his identity, personality, priorities)?

- How does he want me to *live* differently?

_____

_____

_____

_____

_____

_____

_____

_____

_____

_____

_____

_____

_____

_____

_____

_____

_____

_____

_____

DVD NOTES

If you are watching the accompanying *Beginning in Christ Together* DVD, write down what you sense God is saying to you through the speaker. (If you'd like to hear a sample of the DVD teaching segment, go to www.lifetogether.com/ExperiencingChristTogether.)

_____

_____

_____

_____

_____

_____

_____

_____

_____

_____

_____

_____

_____

_____

_____

_____

_____

_____

_____

_____

_____

_____

_____

_____

_____

_____

_____

SESSION 4 THE SERVANT

Tracy stared into an empty refrigerator. Even with two incomes, money was tight for her family of three.

"Darryl, if we're going to eat this weekend, I'm going to need about $80 by then," she told her husband.

"Okay, I'll get you the money somehow, even if we have to skip paying a bill."

God would provide. He'd done it before. But how would he do it this time?

Neither Tracy nor Darryl wanted to tell anyone. It was tough to admit they needed help. Although they'd recently joined a small group with friends from Tracy's office, they told the group almost nothing about their financial struggles.

Other group members had enough trouble of their own, didn't they? One couple had just learned their baby would be born with birth defects. Another couple had a son going through legal problems. So Tracy and Darryl stayed silent.

Days later, they hosted their group for a barbecue at their house. As the group prepared the food they'd brought, one of the members, Susan, opened Tracy and Darryl's refrigerator to get something.

No milk. No bread. Nothing.

Susan had never seen a refrigerator that bare. But she did understand what it was like to overcome financial hardships. The empty refrigerator brought back memories of her own family's struggles and of the friends who helped them through.

"They'd just show up at the house with laundry detergent, milk, or $100 worth of groceries," Susan said. She believed God wanted her group to do the same thing for Tracy and Darryl.

Together, six members went food shopping. They had a blast choosing what to get, laughing their way through the store. Tracy was stunned when they arrived at her house with bags of groceries.

Tracy and Darryl weren't the only ones who benefited from the group's generosity. The whole group grew closer from the experience. They got to be the hands and feet of Christ, and they haven't been the same since.

CONNECTING WITH GOD'S FAMILY   10 min.

For an opening prayer, have a few people thank God for something he's doing in their lives. You might follow this time of prayer by playing a song from a LIFE TOGETHER Worship DVD to help everyone focus on God. Then choose one of the following two questions:

1. Share one word that describes where you are at the moment (such as tired, overwhelmed, relaxed, ready-to-go, hungry, angry, sad, grateful). Please don't comment, question, or interrupt until everyone is done. Then have one or several people pray for your time together. Ask God to meet each of you right where you are.

Or,

2. Sit with your spiritual partner(s). What have you been learning from God during your personal time with him? You might share something from your journal.

GROWING TO BE LIKE CHRIST   40 min.

Like our society, the ancient world measured people by their social status, not their hearts. To be a servant was to be a nobody. So when the New Testament writers said the Son of God took on "the very nature of a servant" (Philippians 2:7), they meant to shock their readers. It was like saying the world's richest man had decided to become a day laborer.

But the writers of the New Testament were only repeating Jesus' own ideas. In the hours before he was arrested and executed, he gave his disciples their final briefing. He showed them the deepest place of his heart. And true to form, he shocked them.

3. Read John 13:1–17. Why did Jesus wash the disciples' feet?

4. What is the relationship between love and serving (verse 1)?

5. How was what Jesus knew about himself (verse 3) relevant to his decision to serve?

6. What similar things do you think Christians should know about themselves?

7. Why would knowing this about ourselves motivate us to serve others?

8. Why did Peter resist letting Jesus wash his feet (verses 6, 8)?

9. Foot washing was a menial and disgusting act of service. What is a modern act of service that would feel disgusting or humiliating for you? (For example, loving an unlovable person at your work or doing something your spouse loves but you hate.) Explain why.

10. Jesus says we should use foot washing as the standard for our treatment of each other. What do you think it would look like for you to follow this standard in your group?

What would it look like in your family or your church?

11. Conventional wisdom warns us that living like a servant is crazy. If we focus on everybody else's needs, who will look after our needs? We'll be doormats. People will take advantage of us. We know this. Jesus knew it too—he was, after all, heading open-eyed into crucifixion. How do you think Jesus would address this concern about our needs?

FOR DEEPER STUDY

What do we need to understand about ourselves and the Father if we are to be full-hearted servants (Luke 12:22–34; Matthew 6:1–4; 7:9–12)?

Philippians 2:1–11 describes the extent of Jesus' servanthood. Why would Jesus limit himself for our sake? To what extent does that motivate you to be less concerned about your position in life and more concerned about serving others?

Why does Jesus use the word "love" to describe the heart of a servant (1 Peter 1:22; John 13:34–35; 15:12–13, 17)?

How does 1 Corinthians 13:4–8 help you understand what serving someone actually looks like?

How does a servant's heart affect marriage and other relationships (Colossians 3:18–25; Ephesians 5:21–33)?

DEVELOPING YOUR GIFTS TO SERVE OTHERS   15 min.

Jesus wants us to care for each other's basic human needs, even when receiving that care feels embarrassing (as it did for Peter), and even when giving that care stretches our love muscles. Right here in this group is a great place to begin developing a servant's heart. People in your group may have all sorts of needs, such as:

☐ Child care during meetings or at other times
☐ Transportation
☐ Help finding a job
☐ Emotional or practical support while caring for an aging or ill relative
☐ Practical help when a friend or family member is hospitalized
☐ Encouragement in the face of trials
☐ Help with household tasks during a busy season of life
☐ Companionship during loneliness or loss

In addition, you may know members of your church who are ill, in a nursing home, jobless, or in some other situation that requires extra care. You may have a neighbor who could use a batch of cookies, or your church may have a ministry to the poor. You are the church—your pastor can't do everything! And while pastors routinely make hospital visits (for example), you can't imagine how it affects someone when a whole group shows up in his hospital room.

12. The first step in serving others is identifying needs. If your group feels comfortable discussing needs of group members or those outside the group, simply appoint someone to write down ideas. Take ten minutes to share your own needs or needs of those you know. Then ask for volunteers to organize the group in addressing one or more needs on your list.

Keep it simple and assign someone to plan it over the course of the next two to three weeks. You'll find the entire process, from start to finish, to be a great bonding experience. (Check out www.lifetogether.com for stories of other groups who have done this.) Also, write down your group's service project on your Personal Health Plan on page 22.

13. A practical and fun exercise is "secret servants." On slips of paper, have each person write his or her name and (optionally) one personal need. Put all the names in a hat, and let everyone draw out a name. You will be that person's "secret servant" for one week. (If you get your name or your spouse's, draw another name.) Respond to that person's need, or ask God to show you how to serve that person in a simple, creative way. At the beginning of your next meeting, see if anybody could figure out who they were paired up with.

 SURRENDERING YOUR LIFE FOR GOD'S PLEASURE   15 min.

14. Surrendering your life to God isn't easy. The hard part today may be admitting you need help from others, or it may be making space in your life to care for someone else's needs. Take a moment of quiet reflection and write your thoughts on the journal page for this session (page 55). Simply finish this sentence: "Father, I need your help today with . . ."

If time allows and you are willing, share what you wrote with your spiritual partner, a friend, or your spouse. The Bible says bearing one another's burdens is a pathway to healing and hope (Galatians 6:2). Take a risk!

15. Close by praying briefly for those whose needs were shared in this session. Pray also for the impact you will have in the lives you serve. For a change of pace, stand in a circle and hold hands to pray.

STUDY NOTES

Passover (John 13:1). Passover was a meal ceremony. In it, the Jews remembered how God protected their ancestors from a plague and freed them from slavery in Egypt. The plague was God's judgment on the Egyptians for Pharaoh's refusal to free the Israelites. It struck every firstborn child in Egypt, except those in homes where lamb's blood was spread on the doorposts. In an act of grace, God passed over the Jewish homes marked with blood. For centuries after, Jews celebrated Passover by eating sacrificial lamb and other special foods. (Today they don't sacrifice a lamb.)

Jesus held his last meal with his followers on the evening before Passover. He used this meal to teach some key things about his mission and theirs. With bread and wine, he taught them that his body and blood would be the final Passover sacrifice, freeing God's people from slavery to sin and death. By washing their feet, he taught them that his life and death were supreme acts of service, and that they should model their lives after his.

Read Exodus 12:1–13:10 for the fullest understanding of Passover.

Jesus knew (13:3). He knew his purpose stretched beyond the menial and even painful acts of service his Father asked from him. He was secure with his Father, so social status didn't matter to him. His purpose was far greater than serving himself and getting his own needs met. Because God is love, it is his nature to serve.

Wash his disciples' feet (13:5). Because people wore sandals and the streets were dirty and often littered with animal waste, it was common practice for the lowest slave in the house to wash the feet of those who entered. Peter couldn't bear to see his Lord do such a demeaning task. Was it degrading to assume such a position? Or did Jesus redefine greatness and lowliness by this act?

You do not realize now what I am doing (13:7). The disciples did not yet understand the deep intensity with which Jesus loved them. Washing their feet was nothing compared to what he would do for them in a few hours—endure a slow and violent death.

A person who has had a bath needs only to wash his feet (13:10). The "bath" is repentance and the full cleansing from sin that accompanies it. (Baptism, a ritual bath, represents this cleansing.) But even committed disciples, who are essentially cleansed from sin through faith in Christ, still sin. Therefore, confession and repentance need to be regular habits for us. Washing each other's feet thus involves not only caring for each other's physical needs, but also helping one another continually cleanse our lives from clinging sins.

PRAYER AND PRAISE REPORT

Briefly share your prayer requests with the large group, making notations below. Then gather in small groups of two to four to pray for each other.

Date: _____

Prayer Requests

_____

_____

_____

_____

_____

_____

_____

_____

_____

Praise Report

_____

_____

_____

_____

_____

_____

_____

_____

_____

Use this page to write out your prayers, your thoughts about your daily Bible reading, or your meditations on a verse from the passage you have already studied. Below are some suggested verses for meditation. The Bible Reading Plan is on page 99.

For Meditation: John 13:3–5 or 13:13–16

For Gospel Reading:

- What do I *learn* from the life of Christ (his identity, personality, priorities)?

- How does he want me to *live* differently?

_____

_____

_____

_____

_____

_____

_____

_____

_____

_____

_____

_____

_____

_____

_____

_____

_____

_____

DVD NOTES

If you are watching the accompanying *Beginning in Christ Together* DVD, write down what you sense God is saying to you through the speaker. (If you'd like to hear a sample of the DVD teaching segment, go to www.lifetogether.com/ExperiencingChristTogether.)

_____

_____

_____

_____

_____

_____

_____

_____

_____

_____

_____

_____

_____

_____

_____

_____

_____

_____

_____

_____

_____

_____

_____

_____

_____

_____

THE SAVIOR

When Rachel started visiting a church, she was looking for something to help her handle stress. She was upper management in a corporation with hundreds of employees, and the long hours and tough decisions were getting to her.

Because several of her close friends had recently moved away, Rachel also appreciated the chance to make new friends at the church. She volunteered with one of the ministry programs and joined a small group. Eventually she was praying regularly with some other women—the last thing on earth she thought she'd ever do. Her idea of God was more like the life force of the universe than what the other women believed in.

But as they got to know each other, Rachel opened up about the anxiety that plagued her. She feared making costly mistakes at work. She feared spending her life alone. She feared she was in the wrong career but didn't know what to do instead. She feared trying to survive with less than a six-figure salary.

One day, one of the other women talked about sin in her own life. Sin. It dawned on Rachel that for her, anxiety might be a sin. Maybe God was this personal Being the others believed in. And maybe Rachel's frantic efforts to figure life out on her own was a slap in God's face. A sin. Rachel had wanted a God to save her from stress, but now she thought maybe she needed a God to save her from sin.

CONNECTING WITH GOD'S FAMILY   10 min.

To fulfill any of God's other purposes, we need to Connect—first with God, and then with his family. We hope this study guide is helping you begin or deepen an intimate connection with Christ. We also hope you've been deepening your relationships with one another.

It's possible to have close friendships built around something other than Christ. In fact, God doesn't want you to restrict yourself

to Christian friends—he wants you to share your life broadly. Yet Christ-centered friendships are like none other. His power works within and among you. This session will focus on the core event that makes Christ-centered friendships possible. Choose one of these opening questions:

1. How has your week been? Choose one of the following, and tell why you chose it in two sentences or less. (Not five sentences—you talkative ones know who you are!)

   ☐ Gold Medal Week
   ☐ Silver Medal Week
   ☐ Bronze Medal Week
   ☐ Booby Prize Week

   Or,

2. Check in with your spiritual partner(s). What has happened in your personal time with God this week? How can your partner pray for you?

 GROWING TO BE LIKE CHRIST   40 min.

The disciples met Jesus as Teacher and Healer. As they followed him, he became their Shepherd. On the night before his death, he revealed himself as Servant and Friend. But a few hours later, when the authorities arrested Jesus, his disciples fled.

They believed he was the Messiah—the King of God's kingdom, the One who was leading the way in doing what the Father wanted done. But they still didn't understand what being the Messiah really meant. They wanted a military savior who would overthrow the Romans by force. They thought Rome was the enemy. All their assumptions—about who the enemy was, what victory involved, and what the kingdom would look like—were turned upside down when Jesus demonstrated what *Messiah* and *Savior* meant.

3. Sometimes we say too lightly, "Jesus died for my sins." It's worthwhile to do something unusual to let that amazing, bloody event affect your heart anew. For the next fifteen minutes, read the story of Jesus' death aloud like a play. Ask for volunteers to read the roles of:

- Narrator (N)
- Jesus (J)
- Pilate, the Roman governor (P)
- Voice of various individuals (V)

The entire group will read the lines of the Crowd so you can all experience the truth that you too were there when Christ was rejected and killed.

N: When he had finished praying, Jesus left with his disciples and crossed the Kidron Valley. On the other side there was an olive grove, and he and his disciples went into it.

Now Judas, who betrayed him, knew the place, because Jesus had often met there with his disciples. So Judas came to the grove, guiding a detachment of soldiers and some officials from the chief priests and Pharisees. They were carrying torches, lanterns and weapons. Jesus, knowing all that was going to happen to him, went out and asked them,

J: Who is it you want?

Crowd: Jesus of Nazareth.

J: I am he.

N: (And Judas the traitor was standing there with them.) When Jesus said, "I am he," they drew back and fell to the ground. Again he asked them,

J: Who is it you want?

Crowd: Jesus of Nazareth.

J: I told you that I am he. If you are looking for me, then let these men go.

N: This happened so that the words he had spoken would be fulfilled: "I have not lost one of those you gave me." Then Simon Peter, who had a sword, drew it and struck the high priest's servant, cutting off his right ear. (The servant's name was Malchus.) Jesus commanded Peter,

J: Put your sword away! Shall I not drink the cup the Father has given me?

N: Then the detachment of soldiers with its commander and the Jewish officials arrested Jesus. They bound him and brought him first to Annas, who was the father-in-law of Caiaphas, the high priest that year. Caiaphas was the one who had advised the Jews that it would be good if one man died for the people. The high priest questioned Jesus about his disciples and his teaching.

J: I have spoken openly to the world. I always taught in synagogues or at the temple, where all the Jews come together. I said nothing in secret. Why question me? Ask those who heard me. Surely they know what I said.

N: When Jesus said this, one of the officials nearby struck him in the face.

V: Is this the way you answer the high priest?

J: If I said something wrong, testify as to what is wrong. But if I spoke the truth, why did you strike me?

N: Then the Jews led Jesus from Caiaphas to the palace of the Roman governor. By now it was early morning, and to avoid ceremonial uncleanness the Jews did not enter the palace; they wanted to be able to eat the Passover. So Pilate came out to them and asked,

P: What charges are you bringing against this man?

Crowd: If he were not a criminal, we would not have handed him over to you.

P: Take him yourselves and judge him by your own law.

Crowd: But we have no right to execute anyone.

N: This happened so that the words Jesus had spoken indicating the kind of death he was going to die would be fulfilled. Pilate then went back inside the palace, summoned Jesus and asked him,

P: Are you the king of the Jews?

J: Is that your own idea, or did others talk to you about me?

P: Am I a Jew? It was your people and your chief priests who handed you over to me. What is it you have done?

J: My kingdom is not of this world. If it were, my servants would fight to prevent my arrest by the Jews. But now my kingdom is from another place.

P:	You are a king, then!
J:	You are right in saying I am a king. In fact, for this reason I was born, and for this I came into the world, to testify to the truth. Everyone on the side of truth listens to me.
P:	What is truth?
N:	. . . Pilate asked. With this he went out again to the Jews and said,
P:	I find no basis for a charge against him. But it is your custom for me to release to you one prisoner at the time of the Passover. Do you want me to release "the king of the Jews"?
N:	They shouted back,
Crowd:	No, not him! Give us Barabbas!
N:	Now Barabbas had taken part in a rebellion. Then Pilate took Jesus and had him flogged. The soldiers twisted together a crown of thorns and put it on his head. They clothed him in a purple robe and went up to him again and again, saying,
Crowd:	Hail, king of the Jews!
N:	And they struck him in the face. Once more Pilate came out and said to the Jews,
P:	Look, I am bringing him out to you to let you know that I find no basis for a charge against him.
N:	When Jesus came out wearing the crown of thorns and the purple robe, Pilate said to them,
P:	Here is the man!
N:	As soon as the chief priests and their officials saw him, they shouted,
Crowd:	Crucify! Crucify!
N:	But Pilate answered,
P:	You take him and crucify him. As for me, I find no basis for a charge against him.
Crowd:	We have a law, and according to that law he must die, because he claimed to be the Son of God.
N:	When Pilate heard this, he was even more afraid, and he went back inside the palace.

P: Where do you come from?

N: . . . he asked Jesus, but Jesus gave him no answer.

P: Do you refuse to speak to me? Don't you realize I have power either to free you or to crucify you?

N: Jesus answered,

J: You would have no power over me if it were not given to you from above. Therefore the one who handed me over to you is guilty of a greater sin.

N: From then on, Pilate tried to set Jesus free, but the Jews kept shouting,

Crowd: If you let this man go, you are no friend of Caesar. Anyone who claims to be a king opposes Caesar.

N: When Pilate heard this, he brought Jesus out and sat down on the judge's seat at a place known as the Stone Pavement (which in Aramaic is Gabbatha). It was the day of Preparation of Passover Week, about the sixth hour.

P: Here is your king,

N: . . . Pilate said to the Jews. But they shouted,

Crowd: Take him away! Take him away! Crucify him!

P: Shall I crucify your king?

Crowd: We have no king but Caesar.

N: Finally Pilate handed him over to them to be crucified. So the soldiers took charge of Jesus. Carrying his own cross, he went out to the place of the Skull (which in Aramaic is called Golgotha). Here they crucified him, and with him two others—one on each side and Jesus in the middle.

Pilate had a notice prepared and fastened to the cross. It read: JESUS OF NAZARETH, THE KING OF THE JEWS. Many of the Jews read this sign, for the place where Jesus was crucified was near the city, and the sign was written in Aramaic, Latin and Greek. The chief priests of the Jews protested to Pilate,

Crowd: Do not write "The King of the Jews," but that this man claimed to be king of the Jews.

P: What I have written, I have written.

N: When the soldiers crucified Jesus, they took his clothes, dividing them into four shares, one for each of them, with the undergarment remaining. This garment was seamless, woven in one piece from top to bottom.

V: Let's not tear it. Let's decide by lot who will get it.

N: This happened that the scripture might be fulfilled which said, "They divided my garments among them and cast lots for my clothing."

N: Near the cross of Jesus stood his mother, his mother's sister, Mary the wife of Clopas, and Mary Magdalene. When Jesus saw his mother there, and the disciple whom he loved standing nearby, he said to his mother,

J: Dear woman, here is your son,

N: . . . and to the disciple,

J: Here is your mother.

N: From that time on, this disciple took her into his home. Later, knowing that all was now completed, and so that the Scripture would be fulfilled, Jesus said,

J: I am thirsty.

N: A jar of wine vinegar was there, so they soaked a sponge in it, put the sponge on a stalk of the hyssop plant, and lifted it to Jesus' lips. When he had received the drink, Jesus said,

J: It is finished.

N: With that, he bowed his head and gave up his spirit.

Now it was the day of Preparation, and the next day was to be a special Sabbath. Because the Jews did not want the bodies left on the crosses during the Sabbath, they asked Pilate to have the legs broken and the bodies taken down. The soldiers therefore came and broke the legs of the first man who had been crucified with Jesus, and then those of the other. But when they came to Jesus and found that he was already dead, they did not break his legs. Instead, one of the soldiers pierced Jesus' side with a spear, bringing a sudden flow of blood and water. The man who saw it has given testimony, and his testimony is true. He knows that he tells the truth, and he testifies so that you also may believe.

John 18:1–14, 19–23, 28–40; 19:1–35

4. As you read this story, what was most significant to you? What words and phrases stood out?

5. Why did Jesus stop Peter from trying to prevent Jesus' arrest (18:10–11)?

6. Why did Jesus refuse to answer the high priest's questions (18:19–24)?

7. Jesus said he came into the world "to testify to the truth" (18:37). To what truth did he testify?

8. What did Jesus understand about power that Pilate didn't (19:10–11)?

9. Go back over the words of the crowd. (For example, "Crucify him!" "We have no king but Caesar.") How do these reflect common human attitudes toward God?

10. "King" is an often repeated word in this passage. The events hinge on whether and how Jesus is King. What do you think Pilate's idea of a king is? What kind of king is Jesus?

11. John doesn't give many details about the violence and agony Jesus endured. Why do you suppose he doesn't?

12. On page 69, read the study note for Jesus' words, "It is finished." What are the implications of this statement for you personally?

FOR DEEPER STUDY

At the meal before his arrest, Jesus used the food on the table to explain his death. Read Matthew 26:26–29. How did he explain his death? How do you understand his words about the bread and the cup?

Jesus went to the cross on purpose, to be executed in place of the guilty. How does his act affect the way God views and treats you if you have placed your faith in Jesus? See Romans 5:1–11. How does this truth make you want to respond to God? How does it make you want to respond to others?

How is Jesus' death supposed to affect the way we live? See Romans 6:1–4, 11–14.

To understand more fully what Jesus' death accomplished, see Romans 3:9–26; Hebrews 9:11–26; and Leviticus 16:1–28.

SHARING YOUR LIFE MISSION EVERY DAY   5 min.

13. If this study has helped you deepen your connection with Christ and one another, we encourage you to share it with others. The best way to plant the good news of Christ deep in your heart is to give it away. Maybe you have one friend with whom you could meet one-on-one to go through this study.

Or, maybe your pastor could use your help in starting new small groups. If so, you (and maybe a partner) could take a six-week break from your group to lead a new group through this study. If you don't want a vacation from your group, you can even come infrequently or double up for a few weeks. It doesn't even have to be an official "group"—the Bible says that Jesus is present wherever two or three of his people are gathered (Matthew 18:20). At www.lifetogether.com you can find stories of other groups that have taken this step of faith.

In Jesus' kingdom, the more you give away, the more you have. Take a moment to think about how you can give away what you've learned in this group.

14. The volunteers who are coordinating your party (from session 2) and/or your service efforts (from session 4) may take a few minutes to update the group on plans and recruit any needed help.

SURRENDERING YOUR LIFE FOR GOD'S PLEASURE   5 min.

15. How can the group pray for you this week? What would you like to ask from Christ the Savior?

16. Communion, or the Lord's Supper, is something Christians do to remember and honor what Jesus did for us through his death on the cross. How does your church celebrate Communion? Consider planning a time to share Communion together. Ask your pastor for guidance, and see www.lifetogether.com for a free download of instructions for sharing Communion in a small group.

17. Someone in your group may never have made an authentic connection with Christ as Savior. This would be a good time to let people think about it without putting pressure on anyone. If you want to start a connection with Jesus, here's a prayer you can pray now silently, or later on your own or with a friend:

    Jesus, I want you to be part of my life as my Teacher, Healer, Shepherd, Servant, and Savior. I want to be your disciple and live the way you want me to live. Please forgive me for a lifetime of trying to live without you. Help me to believe you love me and have good purposes for my life. Connect me with friends who can help me know you better. Amen.

    If you already have a connection with Christ, use these quiet moments to thank him for what he's done for you. Don't worry about anyone or anything else but God. The Bible says to draw near to God and he will draw near to you.

STUDY NOTES

The meal that began with the foot washing was over. Jesus went with his closest friends to an olive grove to pray. He knew Judas already had slipped out to tell the authorities they could arrest him there. Before long, Judas and the arresting officers arrived.

I am he (John 18:5, 6, 8). The Greek grammar of this phrase was unusual. Said this way, the phrase signified divinity to both Jews and non-Jews. The Lord used it in Exodus 3:14. The goddess Isis used it in a sacred poem of her cult. It's not surprising that the Jewish and Roman guards fell to the ground in terror when they heard a mortal utter these words.

Caiaphas (18:28). The Jewish high priest. John's gospel tells us little about what happened when the Jewish authorities interrogated Jesus. The other three Gospels say the authorities found Jesus guilty of blasphemy. Blasphemy was punishable by having the community stone the condemned person to death. The Romans officially outlawed the Jews from carrying out death sentences (see verse 31), but unofficially they sometimes looked the other way. However, the Jewish authorities didn't want Jesus to become a martyr like John the Baptist. They wanted the Roman governor to execute him as a political criminal.

The Roman governor (18:28). During his ten-year stint as prefect of Judea, the Jews accused Pontius Pilate of murder, robbery, and other crimes. They rioted when he had soldiers parade through the streets of Jerusalem with an image of the emperor, which the Jews regarded as an idol. His subjects loathed him, and Rome would discipline him if they rioted either in favor of or in opposition to a supposed Messiah. He couldn't afford to lose the support of the Jewish authorities either.

King of the Jews (18:33). From the Roman point of view, this was a political title. The Messiah/Anointed One/King of the Jews was expected to lead an armed rebellion to eject the Romans from Israel. Because neither Pilate nor the Jewish authorities understood what the King and his kingdom were really about, Jesus couldn't answer Pilate's question with a simple yes or no.

Flogged (19:1). A brutal whipping with metal-tipped thongs.

Crucify (19:6). Crucifixion was the most feared form of execution the Romans had devised, and they used it on criminals they especially wanted to degrade. The victim took hours to die while the position of his body forced him to struggle for every breath. Deuteronomy 21:23 declared that "anyone who is hung on a tree is under God's curse," and the Jewish authorities wanted their people to believe that God had cursed Jesus.

Disciple whom Jesus loved (19:26). The apostle John. Jesus sent his mother to live with John possibly because her own family was distancing itself from a woman who believed her condemned son was the Messiah.

It is finished (19:30). A single word in Greek: *tetelestai!* It is a shout of triumph: "It is accomplished!" Archaeologists have found invoices inscribed on pottery from the first century AD. Many have *tetelestai* written across them, signifying, "Paid in full." Jesus deliberately took our sin upon himself. In his final moments, he declared that he had paid the full price of our debt and accomplished his mission on earth.

PRAYER AND PRAISE REPORT

Briefly share your prayer requests with the large group, making notations below. Then gather in small groups of two to four to pray for each other.

Date: _____

Prayer Requests

_____

_____

_____

_____

_____

_____

_____

_____

_____

Praise Report

_____

_____

_____

_____

_____

_____

_____

_____

_____

REFLECTIONS

Use this page to write out your prayers, your thoughts about your daily Bible reading, or your meditations on a verse from the passage you have already studied. Below are some suggested verses for meditation. The Bible Reading Plan is on page 99.

For Meditation: John 19:8–11 or 19:28–30

For Gospel Reading:

- What do I *learn* from the life of Christ (his identity, personality, priorities)?

- How does he want me to *live* differently?

_____

_____

_____

_____

_____

_____

_____

_____

_____

_____

_____

_____

_____

_____

_____

_____

_____

_____

_____

DVD NOTES

If you are watching the accompanying *Beginning in Christ Together* DVD, write down what you sense God is saying to you through the speaker. (If you'd like to hear a sample of the DVD teaching segment, go to www.lifeto-gether.com/ExperiencingChristTogether.)

THE RISEN LORD

Ken looked like a deer caught in the headlights that evening as Todd walked up and asked if he could help in any way. Ken was paralyzed by fear. His wife had kicked him out of the house, and now with no place to stay, he was standing on the church property looking for direction. Ken knew about Jesus but didn't know him personally.

Ken was a really good guy. He was a firefighter and handy around the house. He loved to help others. He loved his wife and was willing to make any accommodations necessary to meet her desires and save his marriage. Todd was taken back by his willingness to serve her. Yet Ken's marriage was falling apart, and no matter how hard he tried, he couldn't convince his wife to hang in there with him.

That night, in tears, Ken gave his life to Christ. He couldn't muster up enough power to change his life. He surrendered all to the resurrection power of Jesus Christ. Ken and his wife joined a small group and recently wrote Todd a card to tell him about the changes God has made in their lives.

 CONNECTING WITH GOD'S FAMILY — 10 min.

1. In one sentence or less (not two or five), tell why you are grateful for this group. Simply finish one of these sentences:

☐ Because [name of person and what he or she did] . . .
☐ I have learned . . .
☐ If I hadn't been here, I wouldn't have done . . .
☐ Life would still be . . .

Or,

2. Check in with your spiritual partner(s). What's happening in your personal time with God?

GROWING TO BE LIKE CHRIST

40 min.

When Jesus died, his disciples thought their dreams of a Messiah-King and God's kingdom died with him. When they saw him alive again, they knew everything he had told them—everything they hadn't understood before—was true.

The resurrection isn't just a Hollywood ending to a nice story. It's an invitation for us to start fresh, to take Christ's promise of new life seriously. Jesus is alive here, now, today. He has defeated death, and now all authority is in his hands. That changes everything!

3. Read John 20:1–9. Imagine yourself in Peter's place. What do you hear?

What do you see?

4. Read John 20:10–18. What do you make of the fact that Mary didn't recognize Jesus until he said her name?

5. What is significant to you in Jesus' words: "I am returning to my Father and your Father, to my God and your God" (verse 17)?

6. Read John 20:19–23. Why do you suppose Jesus made a point of showing the disciples his wounded hands and side?

7. From what you've read in John 20:1–23, how was the resurrected Jesus different from a ghost or a spirit being on a higher spiritual plane?

8. As soon as Jesus showed up alive, he started giving powerful words to his followers. What is significant to you in the following?

"Peace be with you" (John 20:19, 21; compare John 16:33).

"As the Father has sent me, I am sending you" (John 20:21).

"Receive the Holy Spirit. If you forgive anyone his sins, they are forgiven; if you do not forgive them, they are not forgiven" (John 20:22–23).

9. God's final purpose for you is to "Surrender Your Life for God's Pleasure." He made you so he could delight in you, and draw you into the intimate relationship that the Father, the Son

(Jesus), and the Holy Spirit have had for all eternity. Surrender involves worshiping the Risen Lord with everything in you, as Mary did when she saw him alive again. It means giving up doing life your way and, instead, doing life God's way with everything you have! The more you surrender, the more you live moment by moment in God's kingdom.

The resurrection affects you in at least four ways:

- Jesus' resurrection demonstrates that he really is the Son of God (Romans 1:4).
- His resurrection frees you from having to fear death (Hebrews 2:14–15; 1 Corinthians 15:54–58). Death has no final hold over you. You have nothing to fear from aging, disease, or failure either, because none of those are final. You're going to live eternally with God and his people. You don't need to fear the eternal separation from God that awaits those who reject him (Matthew 25:31–46).
- His resurrection frees you from spiritual death (Ephesians 2:1–7). You can have an intimate connection with God right now.
- His resurrection gives you the chance to live with his life in you, free of the sinful compulsions that would otherwise enslave you (Romans 6:5–14). If you cooperate, you have access to the power to live increasingly free from sin.

Which one of these effects of the resurrection most motivates you to surrender to God in your current situation?

10. Take a moment to write down how you would complete this sentence:

A person or area of my life I want to surrender to the Risen Lord is _____

_____

_____

_____.

If you're concerned about privacy, write an abbreviation only you will understand. On your Personal Health Plan on page 22, you may make a note of your answer.

Jesus doesn't just offer us eternal life after death. He offers us new life, here and now. We live each day as disciples of Jesus with resurrection power through the Holy Spirit (John 20:22). We sell the gospel short if we forget how it will change our lives while we still live on this earth.

FOR DEEPER STUDY

Compare Luke's resurrection account (Luke 24) to John's. What new insights about the resurrected Christ do you get?

For more on the implications of the resurrection, see 1 Corinthians 15 and the other passages listed in question 9 above.

SHARING YOUR LIFE MISSION EVERY DAY   15 min.

11. What's next for your group? Do you want to continue meeting together? If so, the LIFE TOGETHER Agreement on pages 86–87 can help you talk through any changes you might want to make as you move forward. What will you study? Perhaps another book in this series?

12. Is anyone in your group willing to take a six-week break to lead a new group through a LIFE TOGETHER study (see session 5, question 13)? If even one or two of your group members are willing to take up the challenge of leadership, that's something to celebrate!

    Gather around them and ask them to share their greatest fear as they go out to lead. Then pray for them, asking God's abundant blessing on their commitment. And don't worry: they'll be back once the new group gets off the ground.

SURRENDERING YOUR LIFE FOR GOD'S PLEASURE   15 min.

13. How can the group pray for you this week? You don't have to share what you wrote in question 10, but you may.

14. Close by thanking God for what he's done in your group during this study. Sing a worship song about Jesus' resurrection, or pray while you listen to the song on the DVD. An ancient song about the resurrection goes by a Greek name, "The Troparion." It's meant to be said or sung loudly:

> *Christ is risen from the dead*
> *Trampling down death by death*
> *And on those in the tombs bestowing life!*

STUDY NOTES

The tomb (John 20:1). First-century tombs were burial caves. The cave would often be a narrow opening sealed by a stone. Inside could be multiple burial chambers. A body would rest on a bench or in a dug-out niche in the tomb. A tomb was often decorated because it stayed in a family for generations. It would be used over and over again because once the body had decayed and only bones were left, the bones would be transferred to a second burial place called an ossuary, a stone chest with a lid. Jesus' body spent only three days in the tomb and so of course was never transferred to an ossuary.

Strips of linen . . . burial cloth (20:5–7). It was customary to wrap a body in linen strips cemented together with aromatic ointments. Joseph and Nicodemus used about seventy-five pounds of the sticky mixture (19:39–40)—this royal burial would have cost a small fortune. It would also have made it virtually impossible for thieves to unglue the wrappings from the body. One of the ointments, myrrh, "glues linen to the body not less firmly than lead."[1] That's why the sight of the wrappings without the body was so noteworthy.

---

[1]Leon Morris, *The Gospel According to John* (Grand Rapids: Eerdmans, 1971), page 833, note 16. Morris cites the early church leader John Chrysostom for this information.

They still did not understand from Scripture that Jesus had to rise from the dead (20:9). Though Jesus told his disciples about his death and resurrection (Matthew 16:21), they couldn't conceive of it or understand its significance. After his resurrection, they put the pieces together.

Where does Scripture predict Jesus' resurrection? Psalm 16:10 says, "You will not abandon me to the grave, nor will you let your Holy One see decay" (compare Acts 2:25–31). Isaiah 53:11 says, "After the suffering of his soul, he will see the light of life and be satisfied."

With the doors locked (20:19). John presents tantalizing clues about what Jesus' resurrected body was like. Mary didn't recognize him at first, but later did. He was able to get past a locked door. He retained the wounds from his crucifixion. He wasn't a ghost, but his body was definitely different (1 Corinthians 15:51).

If you forgive anyone his sins, they are forgiven (20:23). In Matthew 16:19, Jesus gave Peter and the other disciples the keys to God's kingdom. Whatever they bound on earth would be bound in heaven. He was referring to their evangelistic efforts on earth. He gave them the authority (Matthew 28:18) to preach the gospel and lead others to Christ. Here he reminds them of their duty once again, this time under the guiding power of the Holy Spirit (John 20:22; Acts 1:8).

PRAYER AND PRAISE REPORT

Briefly share your prayer requests with the large group, making notations below. Then gather in small groups of two to four to pray for each other.

Date: _____

Prayer Requests

_____
_____
_____
_____
_____
_____
_____
_____
_____

Praise Report

_____
_____
_____
_____
_____
_____
_____
_____
_____
_____

REFLECTIONS

Use this page to write out your prayers, your thoughts about your daily Bible reading, or your meditations on a verse from the passage you have already studied. Below are some suggested verses for meditation. The Bible Reading Plan is on page 99.

For Meditation: John 20:14–17 or 20:21–22

For Gospel Reading:

- What do I *learn* from the life of Christ (his identity, personality, priorities)?

- How does he want me to *live* differently?

DVD NOTES

If you are watching the accompanying *Beginning in Christ Together* DVD, write down what you sense God is saying to you through the speaker. (If you'd like to hear a sample of the DVD teaching segment, go to www.lifetogether.com/ExperiencingChristTogether.)

_____

_____

_____

_____

_____

_____

_____

_____

_____

_____

_____

_____

_____

_____

_____

_____

_____

_____

_____

_____

_____

_____

_____

_____

_____

_____

FREQUENTLY ASKED QUESTIONS

What do we do on the first night of our group?

Like all fun things in life—have a party! A "get to know you" coffee, dinner, or dessert is a great way to launch a new study. You may want to review the LIFE TOGETHER Agreement (pages 86–87) and share the names of a few friends you can invite to join you. But most importantly, have fun before your study time begins.

Where do we find new members for our group?

This can be troubling, especially for new groups that have only a few people or for existing groups that lose a few people along the way. We encourage you to pray with your group and then brainstorm a list of people from work, church, your neighborhood, your children's school, family, the gym, and so forth. Then have each group member invite several of the people on his or her list. Another good strategy is to ask church leaders to make an announcement or allow a bulletin insert.

No matter how you find members, it's vital that you stay on the lookout for new people to join your group. All groups tend to go through healthy attrition—the result of moves, releasing new leaders, ministry opportunities, and so forth—and if the group gets too small, it could be at risk of shutting down. If you and your group stay open, you'll be amazed at the people God sends your way. The next person just might become a friend for life. You never know!

How long will this group meet?

It's totally up to the group—once you come to the end of this six-week study. Most groups meet weekly for at least the first six weeks, but every other week can work as well. We strongly recommend that the group meet for the first six months on a weekly basis if at all possible. This allows for continuity, and if people miss a meeting they aren't gone for a whole month.

At the end of this study, each group member may decide if he or she wants to continue on for another six-week study. Some groups launch relationships for years to come, and others are stepping-stones into another group experience. Either way, enjoy the journey.

Can we do this study on our own?

Absolutely! This may sound crazy but one of the best ways to do this study is not with a full house but with a few friends. You may choose to gather with one other couple who would enjoy going to the movies or having a quiet dinner and then walking through this study. Jesus will be with you even if there are only two of you (Matthew 18:20).

What if this group is not working for us?

You're not alone! This could be the result of a personality conflict, life stage difference, geographical distance, level of spiritual maturity, or any number of things. Relax. Pray for God's direction, and at the end of this six-week study, decide whether to continue with this group or find another. You don't buy the first car you look at or marry the first person you date, and the same goes with a group. Don't bail out before the six weeks are up—God might have something to teach you. Also, don't run from conflict or prejudge people before you have given them a chance. God is still working in you too!

Who is the leader?

Most groups have an official leader. But ideally, the group will mature and members will rotate the leadership of meetings. We have discovered that healthy groups rotate hosts/leaders and homes on a regular basis. This model ensures that all members grow, give their unique contribution, and develop their gifts. This study guide and the Holy Spirit can keep things on track even when you rotate leaders. Christ has promised to be in your midst as you gather. Ultimately, God is your leader each step of the way.

How do we handle the child care needs in our group?

Very carefully. Seriously, this can be a sensitive issue. We suggest that you empower the group to openly brainstorm solutions. You may try one option that works for a while and then adjust over time. Our favorite approach is for adults to meet in the living room or dining room, and to share the cost of a babysitter (or two) who can be with the kids in a different part of the house. In this way, parents don't have to be away from their children all evening when their children are too young to be left at home. A second option is to use one home for the kids and a second home (close by or a phone call away) for the adults. A third idea is to rotate the responsibility of providing a lesson or care for the children either in the same home or in another home nearby. This can be an incredible blessing for kids. Finally, the most common idea is to decide that you need to have a night to invest in your spiritual lives individually or as a couple, and to make your own arrangements for child care. No matter what decision the group makes, the best approach is to dialogue openly about both the problem and the solution.

To answer your further questions, we have created a website called www.lifetogether.com/ExperiencingChristTogether that can be your small group coach. Here are ten reasons to check out this website:

1. Top twenty questions every new leader asks
2. Common problems most new leaders face and ways to overcome them
3. Seven steps to building a healthy small group in six weeks
4. Free downloadable resources and leadership support
5. Additional leadership training material for every lesson in the EXPERIENCING CHRIST TOGETHER series
6. Ten stories from leaders who successfully completed this study
7. Free chat rooms and bulletin boards
8. Downloadable Health Assessments and Health Plans for individuals or groups
9. A chance to join a community of small group leaders by affinity, geography, or denominational affiliation
10. Best of all, a free newsletter with the best ideas from leaders around the world

LIFE TOGETHER
AGREEMENT

OUR PURPOSE

To transform our spiritual lives by cultivating our spiritual health in a healthy small group community. In addition, we: _____

_____

_____ .

OUR VALUES

Group Attendance	To give priority to the group meeting. We will call or email if we will be late or absent. (Completing the Small Group Calendar on page 88 will minimize this issue.)
Safe Environment	To help create a safe place where people can be heard and feel loved. (Please, no quick answers, snap judgments, or simple fixes.)
Respect Differences	To be gentle and gracious to people with different spiritual maturity, personal opinions, temperaments, or imperfections. We are all works in progress.
Confidentiality	To keep anything that is shared strictly confidential and within the group, and to avoid sharing improper information about those outside the group.
Encouragement for Growth	To be not just takers but givers of life. We want to spiritually multiply our life by serving others with our God-given gifts.
Welcome for Newcomers	To keep an open chair and share Jesus' dream of finding a shepherd for every sheep.
Shared Ownership	To remember that every member is a minister and to ensure that each attender will share a

Rotating Hosts/Leaders and Homes

small team role or responsibility over time. (See Team Roles on pages 89–91.)

To encourage different people to host the group in their homes, and to rotate the responsibility of facilitating each meeting. (See the Small Group Calendar on page 88.)

OUR EXPECTATIONS

• Refreshments/mealtimes _____

• Child care _____

• When we will meet (day of week) _____

• Where we will meet (place) _____

• We will begin at (time)_____ and end at _____

• We will do our best to have some or all of us attend a worship service together. Our primary worship service time will be _____

• Date of this agreement _____

• Date we will review this agreement again _____

• Who (other than the leader) will review this agreement at the end of this study_____

SMALL GROUP
CALENDAR

Planning and calendaring can help ensure the greatest participation at every meeting. At the end of each meeting, review this calendar. Be sure to include a regular rotation of host homes and leaders, and don't forget birthdays, socials, church events, holidays, and mission/ministry projects. Go to www.lifetogether.com for an electronic copy of this form and more than a hundred ideas for your group to do together.

Date	Lesson	Host Home	Dessert/Meal	Leader
Monday, January 15	1	Steve and Laura's	Joe	Bill

TEAM ROLES

The Bible makes clear that every member, not just the small group leader, is a minister in the body of Christ. In a healthy small group, every member takes on some small role or responsibility. It's more fun and effective if you team up on these roles.

Review the team roles and responsibilities below, and have each member volunteer for a role or participate on a team. If someone doesn't know where to serve or is holding back, have the group suggest a team or role. It's best to have one or two people on each team so you have each of the five purposes covered. Serving in even a small capacity will not only help your leader but also will make the group more fun for everyone. Don't hold back. Join a team!

The opportunities below are broken down by the five purposes and then by a *crawl* (beginning step), *walk* (intermediate step), or *run* (advanced step). Try to cover at least the crawl and walk roles, and select a role that matches your group, your gifts, and your maturity. If you can't find a good step or just want to see other ideas, go to www.lifetogether.com and see what other groups are choosing.

Team Roles	Team Player(s)

CONNECTING TEAM (Fellowship and Community Building)

Crawl: Host a social event or group activity
in the first week or two.
_____
_____

Walk: Create a list of uncommitted members
and then invite them to an open house
or group social.
_____
_____

Run: Plan a twenty-four-hour retreat or
weekend getaway for the group.
Lead the Connecting
time each week for the group.
_____
_____

GROWING TEAM (Discipleship and Spiritual Growth)

Crawl: Coordinate the spiritual partners for the   _____
group. Facilitate a three- or four-person   _____
discussion circle during the Bible study
portion of your meeting. Coordinate the
discussion circles.

Walk: Tabulate the Personal Health Assessments   _____
and Health Plans in a summary to let   _____
people know how you're doing as a group.
Encourage personal devotions through group discussions
and pairing up with spiritual (accountability) partners.

Run: Take the group on a prayer walk, or plan   _____
a day of solitude, fasting, or personal retreat. _____

SERVING TEAM (Discovering Your God-Given Design for Ministry)

Crawl: Ensure that every member finds a   _____
group role or team he or she enjoys.   _____

Walk: Have every member take a gift test   _____
(see www.lifetogether.com) and   _____
determine your group's gifts. Plan a
ministry project together.

Run: Help each member decide on a   _____
way to use his or her unique gifts   _____
somewhere in the church.

SHARING TEAM (Sharing and Evangelism)

Crawl: Coordinate the group's Prayer and   _____
Praise Report of friends and family   _____
who don't know Christ.

Walk: Search for group mission opportunities   _____
and plan a cross-cultural group activity.   _____

Run: Take a small-group "vacation" to host a   _____
six-week group in your neighborhood   _____
or office. Then come back together
with your current group.

SURRENDERING TEAM (Surrendering Your Heart to Worship)

Crawl: Maintain the group's Prayer
and Praise Report or journal.

    _____

    _____

Walk: Lead a brief time of worship each
week (at the beginning or end of
your meeting), either a cappella or
using a song from the DVD or the
LIFE TOGETHER Worship DVD/CD.

    _____

    _____

Run: Plan a unique time of worship through
Communion, foot washing, night of
prayer, or nature walking.

    _____

    _____

PERSONAL HEALTH ASSESSMENT

	Just Beginning	Getting Going	Well Developed

CONNECTING WITH GOD AND OTHERS

I am deepening my understanding of and friendship
with God in community with others.   1 2 3 4 5

I am growing in my ability both to share and to
show my love to others.   1 2 3 4 5

I am willing to share my real needs for prayer and
support from others.   1 2 3 4 5

I am resolving conflict constructively and am
willing to forgive others.   1 2 3 4 5

CONNECTING Total _____

GROWING IN YOUR SPIRITUAL JOURNEY

I have a growing relationship with God through regular
time in the Bible and in prayer (spiritual habits).   1 2 3 4 5

I am experiencing more of the characteristics of
Jesus Christ (love, patience, gentleness, courage,
self-control, and so forth) in my life.   1 2 3 4 5

I am avoiding addictive behaviors (food, television,
busyness, and the like) to meet my needs.   1 2 3 4 5

I am spending time with a Christian friend (spiritual partner)
who celebrates and challenges my spiritual growth.   1 2 3 4 5

GROWING Total _____

SERVING WITH YOUR GOD-GIVEN DESIGN

I have discovered and am further developing my
unique God-given design.   1 2 3 4 5

I am regularly praying for God to show me
opportunities to serve him and others.   1 2 3 4 5

I am serving in a regular (once a month or more)
ministry in the church or community.   1 2 3 4 5

I am a team player in my small group by sharing
some group role or responsibility.   1 2 3 4 5

SERVING Total _____

SHARING GOD'S LOVE IN EVERYDAY LIFE

	Just Beginning	Getting Going	Well Developed
I am cultivating relationships with non-Christians and praying for God to give me natural opportunities to share his love.	1 2 3 4 5		
I am praying and learning about where God can use me and my group cross-culturally for missions.	1 2 3 4 5		
I am investing my time in another person or group who needs to know Christ.	1 2 3 4 5		
I am regularly inviting unchurched or unconnected friends to my church or small group.	1 2 3 4 5		

SHARING Total _____

SURRENDERING YOUR LIFE TO GOD

I am experiencing more of the presence and power of God in my everyday life.	1 2 3 4 5		
I am faithfully attending services and my small group to worship God.	1 2 3 4 5		
I am seeking to please God by surrendering every area of my life (health, decisions, finances, relationships, future, and the like) to him.	1 2 3 4 5		
I am accepting the things I cannot change and becoming increasingly grateful for the life I've been given.	1 2 3 4 5		

SURRENDERING Total _____

Connecting	Growing	Serving	Sharing	Surrendering	
20					Well Developed
16					Very Good
12					Getting Going
8					Fair
4					Just Beginning

○ Beginning Assessment Total _____   ☐ Ending Assessment Total _____

PERSONAL HEALTH PLAN

This worksheet could become your single most important feature in this study. On it you can record your personal priorities before the Father. It will help you live a healthy spiritual life, balancing all five of God's purposes.

PURPOSE	PLAN
CONNECT	WHO are you connecting with spiritually?
GROW	WHAT is your next step for growth?
DEVELOP	WHERE are you serving?
SHARE	WHEN are you shepherding another in Christ?
SURRENDER	HOW are you surrendering your heart?

Additional copies of the Personal Health Plan may be downloaded in a larger format at www.lifetogether.com/healthplan.

DATE	MY PROGRESS	PARTNER'S PROGRESS

SAMPLE PERSONAL HEALTH PLAN

This worksheet could become your single most important feature in this study. On it you can record your personal priorities before the Father. It will help you live a healthy spiritual life, balancing all five of God's purposes.

PURPOSE	PLAN
CONNECT	WHO are you connecting with spiritually? *Bill and I will meet weekly by email or phone.*
GROW	WHAT is your next step for growth? *Regular devotions or journaling my prayers 2x/week*
DEVELOP	WHERE are you serving? *Serving in Children's Ministry* *Go through GIFTS class*
SHARE	WHEN are you shepherding another in Christ? *Shepherding Bill at lunch or hosting a starter group in the fall*
SURRENDER	HOW are you surrendering your heart? *Help with our teenager* *New job situation*

DATE	MY PROGRESS	PARTNER'S PROGRESS
3/5	Talked during our group	Figured out our goals together
3/12	Missed our time together	Missed our time together
3/26	Met for coffee and review of my goals	Met for coffee
4/10	Emailed prayer requests	Bill sent me his prayer requests
3/5	Great start on personal journaling	Read Mark 1–6 in one sitting!
3/12	Traveled and not doing well this week	Journaled about Christ as Healer
3/26	Back on track	Busy and distracted; asked for prayer
3/1	Need to call Children's Pastor	
3/26	Group did a serving project together	Agreed to lead group worship
3/30	Regularly rotating leadership	Led group worship—great job!
3/5	Called Jim to see if he's open to joining our group	Wanted to invite somebody, but didn't
3/12	Preparing to start a group this fall	
3/30	Group prayed for me	Told friend something he's learning about Christ
3/5	Overwhelmed but encouraged	Scared to lead worship
3/15	Felt heard and more settled	Issue with wife
3/30	Read book on teens	Glad he took on his fear

JOURNALING 101

Henri Nouwen says effective and lasting ministry *for* God grows out of a quiet place alone *with* God. This is why journaling is so important.

The greatest adventure of our lives is found in the daily pursuit of knowing, growing in, serving, sharing, and worshiping Christ forever. This is the essence of a purposeful life: to see all five biblical purposes fully formed and balanced in our lives. Only then are we "complete in Christ" (Colossians 1:28, NASB).

David poured his heart out to God by writing psalms. The book of Psalms contains many of his honest conversations with God in written form, including expressions of every imaginable emotion on every aspect of his life. Like David, we encourage you to select a strategy to integrate God's Word and journaling into your devotional time. Use any of the following resources:

- Bible
- One-year Bible
- New Testament Bible Challenge Reading Plan (www.lifetogether.com/readingprograms)
- Devotional book
- Topical Bible study plan

Before or after you read a portion of God's Word, speak to God in honest reflection or response in the form of a written prayer. You may begin this time by simply finishing the sentence "Father . . . ," "Yesterday Lord . . . ,"or "Thank you, God, for. . . ." Share with him where you are at the present moment; express your hurts, disappointments, frustrations, blessings, victories, gratefulness. Whatever you do with your journal, make a plan that fits you so you'll have a positive experience. Consider sharing highlights of your progress and experiences with some or all of your group members, especially your spiritual partner(s). You may find they want to join and even encourage you in this journey. Most of all, enjoy the ride and cultivate a more authentic, growing walk with God.

BIBLE READING PLAN

30 Days through the Gospel of Mark

Imagine sitting at the feet of Jesus himself: the Teacher who knows how to live life well, the Savior who died for you, the Lord who commands the universe. Like his first disciples, you can follow him around, watch what he does, listen to what he says, and pattern your life after his.

Find a quiet place, and have ready a notebook or journal in which you can write what you learn and what you want to say back to God. You may also use the Reflections page at the end of each session of this study.

It's helpful to have one or two simple questions in mind to focus your reading. Here are some suggestions:

- What do I *learn* from the life of Christ (his identity, personality, priorities)?
- How does he want me to *live* differently?

When we've sat at the Master's feet like this ourselves, the sense of a real, alive, present Jesus has been breathtaking. We pray you'll have the same experience.

☐ Day 1 Mark 1:1–20
☐ Day 2 Mark 1:21–45
☐ Day 3 Mark 2:1–12
☐ Day 4 Mark 2:13–28
☐ Day 5 Mark 3:1–19
☐ Day 6 Mark 3:20–35
☐ Day 7 Mark 4:1–20
☐ Day 8 Mark 4:21–41
☐ Day 9 Mark 5:1–20
☐ Day 10 Mark 5:21–43
☐ Day 11 Mark 6:1–29
☐ Day 12 Mark 6:30–56
☐ Day 13 Mark 7:1–23
☐ Day 14 Mark 7:24–37
☐ Day 15 Mark 8:1–21

☐ Day 16 Mark 8:22–9:1
☐ Day 17 Mark 9:2–32
☐ Day 18 Mark 9:33–50
☐ Day 19 Mark 10:1–31
☐ Day 20 Mark 10:32–52
☐ Day 21 Mark 11:1–19
☐ Day 22 Mark 11:20–33
☐ Day 23 Mark 12:1–17
☐ Day 24 Mark 12:18–44
☐ Day 25 Mark 13:1–37
☐ Day 26 Mark 14:1–31
☐ Day 27 Mark 14:32–72
☐ Day 28 Mark 15:1–20
☐ Day 29 Mark 15:21–47
☐ Day 30 Mark 16:1–20

LEADING FOR
THE FIRST TIME

- **Sweaty palms are a healthy sign.** The Bible says God is gracious to the humble. Remember who is in control; the time to worry is when you're not worried. Those who are soft in heart (and sweaty-palmed) are those whom God is sure to speak through.

- **Seek support.** Ask your leader, coleader, or close friend to pray for you and prepare with you before the session. Walking through the study will help you anticipate potentially difficult questions and discussion topics.

- **Bring your uniqueness to the study.** Lean into who you are and how God wants you to uniquely lead the study.

- **Prepare. Prepare. Prepare.** Go through the session several times. If you are using the DVD, listen to the teaching segment and Leadership Lifter. Go to www.lifetogether.com and download pertinent files. Consider writing in a journal or fasting for a day to prepare yourself for what God wants to do.

- **Don't wait until the last minute to prepare.**

- **Ask for feedback so you can grow.** Perhaps in an email or on cards handed out at the study, have everyone write down three things you did well and one thing you could improve on. Don't get defensive, but show an openness to learn and grow.

- **Use online resources.** Go to www.lifetogether.com and listen to Brett Eastman share the weekly Leadership Lifter and download any additional notes or ideas for your session. You may also want to subscribe to the Doing Life Together Newsletter and LLT Newsletter. Both can be obtained for free by signing up at www.lifetogether.com/subscribe.

- **Prayerfully consider launching a new group.** This doesn't need to happen overnight, but God's heart is for this to happen over time. Not all

Christians are called to be leaders or teachers, but we are all called to be "shepherds" of a few someday.

- **Share with your group what God is doing in your heart.** God is searching for those whose hearts are fully his. Share your trials and victories. We promise that people will relate.

- **Prayerfully consider whom you would like to pass the baton to next week.** It's only fair. God is ready for the next member of your group to go on the faith journey you just traveled. Make it fun, and expect God to do the rest.

HOSTING AN OPEN HOUSE

If you're starting a new group, try planning an "open house" before your first formal group meeting. Even if you only have two to four core members, it's a great way to break the ice and to consider prayerfully who else might be open to join you over the next few weeks. You can also use this kick-off meeting to hand out study guides, spend some time getting to know each other, discuss each person's expectations for the group, and briefly pray for each other.

A simple meal or good desserts always make a kick-off meeting more fun. After people introduce themselves and share how they ended up being at the meeting (you can play a game to see who has the wildest story!), have everyone respond to a few icebreaker questions: "What is your favorite family vacation?" or "What is one thing you love about your church/our community?" or "What are three things about your life growing up that most people here don't know?" See www.lifetogether.com for more icebreaker ideas.

Next, ask everyone to tell what he or she hopes to get out of the study. You might want to review the LIFE TOGETHER Agreement (pages 86–87) and talk about each person's expectations and priorities.

Finally, set an open chair (maybe two) in the center of your group and explain that it represents someone who would enjoy or benefit from this group but who isn't here yet. Ask people to pray about whom they could invite to join the group over the next few weeks. Hand out postcards (see www.lifetogether.com for examples) and have everyone write an invitation or two. Don't worry about ending up with too many people—you can always have one discussion circle in the living room and another in the dining room after you watch the lesson. Each group could then report prayer requests and progress at the end of the session.

You can skip this kick-off meeting if your time is limited, but you'll experience a huge benefit if you take the time to connect with each other in this way.

Sunday school is one of the best places to begin building community in your church, and the EXPERIENCING CHRIST TOGETHER DVDs and study guides work in concert to help your Sunday school leadership team do it easily and effectively.

Each study guide of the LIFE TOGETHER curriculum includes a companion DVD with today's top Christian leaders speaking to the passage of Scripture under discussion. Here is one way to use the DVD in a Sunday school class:

- Moderator introduction: welcome the class, and read the Scripture passage for the session
- DVD teaching segment: ten to fifteen minutes
- Small group discussion: divide into small groups of eight to twelve and, using the questions from the curriculum, discuss how the passage applies to each person in the class

So often Sunday school consists of the star teacher with little involvement from others. To use the EXPERIENCING CHRIST TOGETHER DVDs effectively means recruiting a host of people to participate in the Sunday school program. We recommend four teams:

Moderators. These are the facilitators or leaders of the class. Their role is to transition the class through each step in the time together. For example, the moderator will welcome the class and open with prayer. In addition, he or she will introduce the DVD segment by reading the Scripture passage for the session. We recommend that you recruit several moderaters. That allows you to rotate the moderators each week. Doing so takes the pressure off people to commit to every week of the class—and it offers more people opportunity for upfront leadership. One church recruited three sets of moderators (a total of six) because the Sunday school leaders wanted to use the curriculum for twelve weeks. They knew that out of twelve weeks, one set of moderators would, likely, burn out; it's difficult for anyone to provide leadership for twelve straight weeks.

Discussion Guides. These are people who lead the follow-up discussion after the DVD teaching segment. If, for example, your Sunday school runs for an hour, you may want to plan on fifteen to twenty minutes for the DVD teaching segment and an additional twenty to thirty minutes in small group discussion afterward. One church recruited many of its seniors to lead the discussion groups. Some of them had felt excluded from ministry, and the role of discussion guide opened the door for them to serve.

Each discussion guide needs only to read through the passage and the questions in each study guide for preparation. After the DVD teaching segment, the moderator of the class asks the discussion guides to stand up. Then, people circle their chairs around each discussion guide. It's an easy way to create small groups each week. You may need to help some groups find more people or other groups to divide once more, if they end up too large. One church asked some of the discussion guides to move their groups into different rooms, because the seniors had a hard time hearing.

Hospitality Coordinators. These are those who oversee the food and drink for the class. Some classes may not provide this, but for those who do, it's important that multiple people join the team, so one or two people don't burn out over the course of the class.

Technical Coordinators. There's nothing worse than a DVD player that doesn't seem to work. Recruit at least one person to oversee making sure the DVD works each week. It's best, though, to recruit two or three people, in order to rotate them throughout the Sunday school series. It's important that the technical team has made sure the DVD player works *before* the class begins.

One church decided to gather all the adult Sunday school classes together for a twelve-week series using the Life Together DVD and study guides. What happened was amazing—instead of Sunday school starting off with 140 people and ending up with half that many at the end of the fall, attendance stayed high the entire time. Instead of one Sunday school class being led by one or two teachers, more than thirty-five people were involved in some kind of leadership—as moderators, discussion guides, hospitality (food) coordinators, or technical coordinators. The fifteen-minute time at the beginning of Sunday school for coffee and snacks (fruit, coffee cake, etc.) proved just as valuable as the content portion!

The fall program gave the church a new vision for how Sunday school can support the larger issue of spiritual formation and life change. For more ideas and practical tools to strengthen your small group ministry, go to www.lifetogethertoday.com.

INTRODUCTION

If your group is new, or even if you haven't been together for a few weeks, we recommend that you plan a kick-off meeting where you will pray, hand out study guides, spend some time getting to know each other, and discuss each person's expectations for the group. A meeting like this is a great way to start a group or step up people's commitments.

Most groups, if reconvened after a short break, will be renewed in seeing each other and open to increasing their commitment as much as 25 percent. We have seen some naturally move to a weekly format, begin doing homework, and commit to daily devotions simply because the leader shared his or her heart. What do you sense God wants from you and your group?

However, if your group is brand new, a simple meal, potluck, or even good desserts make a kick-off meeting more fun. After dessert, have everyone respond to an icebreaker question, such as, "How did you hear of this church, and what's one thing you love about it?" Or, "Tell us three things about your life growing up that most people here don't know."

Then ask everyone to tell what he or she hopes to get out of this study. You might want to review the LIFE TOGETHER Agreement (see pages 86–87) and talk about each person's expectations and priorities. You could discuss whether you want to do Bible study homework before each meeting—homework covering the questions under Growing and/or the For Deeper Study sections. Review the Small Group Calendar on page 88 and talk about who else is willing to open their home or facilitate a meeting.

Finally, cast the vision, as Jesus did, to be inclusive not exclusive. Ask everyone to prayerfully think of people who would enjoy or benefit from a group like this. The beginning of a new study is a great time to welcome a few people into your circle. Have each person share a name or two and either make phone calls the coming week or handwrite invitations or postcards that very night. This will make it fun and also make it happen. At www.lifeto-gether.com we have a free email invitation you may send to every potential member. Don't worry about ending up with too many people—you can always have one discussion circle in the living room and another in the dining room.

SESSION ONE:
THE TEACHER

As a leader, your most important job is to create an atmosphere where people are willing to talk honestly about what Christ's words and actions have to do with them. Especially if your group is new, be available before people arrive so you can greet them at the door. People are naturally nervous at a new group, so a hug or handshake can help put them at ease.

If your group is new and you aren't able to hold a get-to-know-you meeting before you launch into session 1, consider starting this first meeting half an hour early to give people time to socialize without shortchanging your time in the study. For example, you can have social time from 7:00 to 7:30, and by 7:40 you'll gather the group with a prayer. Even if only a few people are seated in the living room by 7:40, ask them to join you in praying for those who are coming and for God to be present among you as you meet. Others will notice you praying and will come and sit down. You may want to softly play music from the DVD or the LIFE TOGETHER Worship DVD/CD series as people arrive and turn up the volume when you are ready to begin. This first night will set the tone for the whole six weeks.

You may ask a few people to come early to help set up, pray, and introduce newcomers to others. Even if everyone is new, they don't know that yet and may be shy when they arrive. You might give people roles like setting up nametags or handing out drinks. This could be a great way to spot a coleader.

Question 1. We've designed this study for both new and established groups, and for both seekers and the spiritually mature. New groups need to invest more time in building relationships with each other, while established groups often want to dig deeper into Bible study and application. Choose whichever icebreaker best fits your group. You should be the first to answer this question while others are thinking about how to respond. Be sure to give everyone a chance to respond to this question, because it's a chance for the group to get to know each other. It's not necessary to go around the circle in order. Just ask for volunteers to respond.

Introduction to the Series. Take a moment after question 1 to orient the group to one principle that undergirds this series: *A healthy small group balances the purposes of the church.* Most small groups emphasize Bible study, fellowship, and prayer. But God has called us to reach out to others as well.

He wants us to *do* what Jesus teaches, not just *learn about* it. You may spend less time in this series studying the Bible than some group members are used to. That's because you'll spend more time doing things the Bible says believers should do.

However, those who like more Bible study can find plenty of it in this series. For Deeper Study provides more passages you can study on the topic of each session. If your group likes to do deeper Bible study, consider having members answer next week's Growing section questions ahead of time as homework. They can even study next week's For Deeper Study passages for homework too. Then, during the Growing portion of your meeting, you can share the high points of what you've learned.

If the five biblical purposes are new to your group, be sure to review them together on pages 8–10 of the Read Me First section.

Question 2. An agreement helps you clarify your group's priorities and cast new vision for what the group can be. Members can imagine what your group could be like if they lived these values. So turn to pages 86–87 and choose one value that you want to emphasize in this study. We've suggested some options. If you choose "rotating leaders," you don't need to invest a lot of time in it now. In session 3 you'll have a chance to plan who will lead each meeting.

Question 3. Have someone read the Bible passage aloud. It's a good idea to ask someone ahead of time, because not everyone is comfortable reading aloud in public. When the passage has been read, ask question 3. *It is not necessary that everyone answer every question in the Bible study.* In fact, a group can become boring if you simply go around the circle and give answers. Your goal is to create a discussion—which means that perhaps only a few people respond to each question and an engaging dialogue gets going. It's even fine to skip some questions in order to spend more time on questions you believe are most important.

Question 4. Everyone needs to understand verse 15. Use the Study Notes to paraphrase this verse in words that make sense to group members. For instance, "The rightful King of the world has arrived. It's now possible to be part of the realm where what makes people truly happy is to do what God wants done. To have this joy, we simply need to change our dead-end ways of thinking (like, 'If I don't look out for myself, nobody else will') and trust the King and his message."

If you have seekers in your group, it's not necessary that they believe this. It's only necessary that they understand the ideas. Can they even imagine being happy in a world where people do what God wants done? It might help to unpack the idea of what God wants done. For instance, God wants us to passionately pursue good for those around us. This is what Christians mean by love: pursuing good for others.

Question 5. We need to change our thinking and direction to the degree that we're not naturally drawn to the things God wants done. If we're naturally drawn to generosity, justice, creativity, and compassion—that's great. But if we're naturally drawn to value possessions or status ahead of people (for example), then we'll need a whole new outlook on what our lives are meant to be about.

Questions 7 and 8. The connection is "authority." Jesus seemed to have the right to teach this radical message about the kingdom. He demonstrated the same kind of authority or right over evil spirits and diseases. Lots of people want to tell us how to live. We need to decide if Jesus has the *right* to tell us how to live.

Question 9. We can believe a set of facts about Jesus (that he's the Son of God, for instance) and still live however we like. Jesus is asking us to believe he has the right, the wisdom, and the love to tell us how to live. This isn't just information that will get us into heaven. This is a new way of life that will get heaven into us—now.

Question 11. We've offered several options for personal time with God. Don't press seekers to do this, but every believer should have a plan for personal time with God. Walk the group through these three options. If group members have never read through the Gospels (Matthew, Mark, Luke, and John), we strongly urge that they take on that option. This will immerse them in the person of Christ for the duration of this study. There's a blank page at the end of every session of this study for them to write down what they discover.

Instead of reading through the Gospels, those who want a deeper topical Bible study could do the For Deeper Study readings each week. It's important that people know this study can adapt to a more spiritually mature group.

For those who have done a lot of Bible study, we encourage the meditation option. Living with one short passage each week can help them move biblical truth from their heads into their hearts and actions. The prayer option—whether five minutes a day or thirty—is valuable for anyone. We strongly suggest those who have never used a personal prayer journal to give it a try.

On the DVD or at www.lifetogether.com/ExperiencingChristTogether, you can find information on how to select a first-time or next-step Bible, ideas on which Bible to pursue, and simple suggestions on how to create your own Bible reference library.

Question 12. For those who haven't done a LIFE TOGETHER study before, spiritual partners will be a new idea. We highly encourage you to try pairs or triplets for six weeks. It's so hard to start a spiritual practice like prayer or consistent Bible reading with no support. A friend makes a huge difference. Partners can check in with each other weekly either at the beginning of your group meetings or outside the meeting.

Question 13. Never pressure a person to pray aloud. That's a sure way to scare someone away from your group. So instead of praying in a circle (which makes it obvious when someone stays silent), allow open time when anyone can pray who wishes to do so. Have someone write down everyone's prayer requests on the Prayer and Praise Report (page 19). If your time is short, consider having people share requests and pray just with their spiritual partners or in smaller circles of three or four.

Question 14. If you have seekers in your group who aren't accustomed to singing worship songs, it might be awkward to sing with the worship song on the DVD. In that case, you may use the DVD-based worship song as a mood setter at the beginning of your meeting and skip worship at the end. Select whichever option best fits your group.

SESSION TWO:
THE HEALER

As you begin, welcome any new people and praise the ones who brought them. Renew the vision to welcome people for one more week and model this if you can. Then have everyone sit back, relax, close their eyes, and listen to one of the songs on the DVD, the LIFE TOGETHER Worship series, or any worship CD. You may want to sing the second time through as a group, or simply take a few moments of silence to focus on God and transition from the distractions of your day to the group.

Questions 1 and 2. Checking in with your spiritual partners (question 2) will be an option in all sessions from now on. You'll need to watch the clock and keep these conversations to ten minutes. If partners want more time together (as is ideal), they can connect before, after, or outside meetings. Give them a two-minute notice and hold to it if you ever want to get them back in the circle! If some group members are absent or newcomers have joined you, you may need to help partnerless people connect with new or temporary partners.

If you prefer (and especially if there are many newcomers), question 1 will always be a lighter icebreaker for the whole group. We encourage you, though, to let partners check in at least every other week so that those relationships grow solid. Please don't miss this opportunity to take your people deeper. Remember that the goal here is "transforming lives through community," and one-on-one time has an enormous return on time spent. In a week or two, you might want to ask the group how their partnerships are going. This will encourage those who are struggling to connect or accomplish their goals.

If newcomers have joined you, take a few minutes before the Growing section to let all members introduce themselves. If you answered question 1 instead of question 2, you could even let each member tell one thing he or she has liked about the group so far, and let the newcomers tell who invited them. The first visit to a new group is scary, so be sure to minimize the inside jokes. Introduce newcomers to some highly relational people when they arrive and partner them with great spiritual partners to welcome them at their first meeting.

Question 3. This study emphasizes observations about Jesus' character. We hope each member will finish this study with a deeper love and respect for who he is as a person. This session highlights his extraordinary compassion, his astonishing authority, his commitment to seek out those who felt unworthy to approach God, and his courage in the face of social disapproval.

We highly recommend that as leader, you read the Study Notes ahead of time and draw the group's attention to anything there that will help them understand the Bible passage.

Question 5. Jesus healed people for at least two reasons. First, he healed them because he felt love and compassion for them. Second, he did it as a sign that God's kingdom was breaking into this fallen world and setting right what was marred by sin. Physical disease and death entered the world because humans rebelled against God. An individual's disease isn't necessarily linked to that individual's sin; rather, diseases as a whole are one result of humanity's sinfulness as a whole. Jesus came as a "physician" for the whole person: body, mind, and spirit. His authority over bodily sickness was meant to demonstrate his authority over all that ails us and our world.

Question 10. This question points toward questions 11 and 12 below.

End your Bible study after half an hour even if you haven't covered all the questions. Questions 11 and 12 are ways to do what Jesus was doing and teaching. James urges us to do what the Word says, not just listen to it (James 1:22–25).

Question 11. The "Circles of Life" represent one of the values of the group agreement: "welcome for newcomers." Some groups fear that newcomers will interrupt the intimacy that members have built over time. However, groups generally gain strength with the infusion of new blood. It's like a river of living water flowing into a stagnant pond. Some groups remain permanently open, while others open periodically, such as at the beginning and ending of a study. Love grows by giving itself away. If your circle becomes too large for easy face-to-face conversations, you can simply form a second discussion circle in another room in your home.

As leader, you should do this exercise yourself in advance and be ready to share the names of the people you're going to invite or connect with. Your modeling is the number-one example that people will follow. Give everyone a few moments in which to write down names before each shares. You might pray for a few of these names on the spot and/or later in the session. Encourage people not to be afraid to ask someone. Almost no one is annoyed to be invited to something! Most people are honored to be asked, even if they can't make it. You may want to hand out invitations and fill them out in the group. Check out the print and email invitations at www.lifetogether.com.

We encourage an outward focus for your group because groups that become too inwardly focused tend to become unhealthy over time. People naturally gravitate to feeding themselves through Bible study, prayer, and social time, so it's usually up to the leader to push them to consider how this inward nourishment can overflow into outward concern for others. Never forget: Jesus came to seek and save the lost and to find a shepherd for every sheep.

Question 12. Make it a priority to have a social event during these six weeks, especially if your group is new. If group members are reluctant to invite outsiders, it can be an event just for members and their families.

If no one volunteers to plan a party—either for group members only or for outsiders as well—don't be discouraged. Who do you think are the one or two party people in your group? They are likely to respond well if you ask them right after your meeting to take on this project and if you ask two people to team up. Another surefire approach is to ask the group who would be two people perfect for this task.

Question 13. There are bound to be people in your group who long for healing, whether physical or emotional, so be sure to save time to pray for each other. Some churches emphasize prayer for healing—if yours does, follow your church's practice in the way you approach this exercise. Other churches prefer to avoid a charismatic flavor in their small groups—if yours has that concern, pray for one another in whatever way seems comfortable. If you're concerned that some members might confuse or try to "fix" others through prayer, pray as a whole group and monitor how people pray. But don't be overly concerned: the very worst that will happen is that someone will pray in a way that distresses someone else, and if that happens you can simply talk to each person privately before your next meeting. As leader, you set the example of how people will pray for each other in your group, and most members will follow your lead.

SESSION THREE: THE SHEPHERD

In order to maximize your time together and honor the diversity of personality types, do your best to begin and end your group on time. You may even want to adjust your starting or stopping time. Don't hesitate to open in prayer even before everyone is seated. This isn't disrespectful of those who are still gathering—it respects those who are ready to begin, and the others won't be offended. An opening prayer can be as simple as, "Welcome, Lord! Help us! Now let's start."

If you've had trouble getting through all of the Bible study questions, consider breaking into smaller circles of four or five people for the Bible study (Growing) portion of your meeting. Everyone will get more "airtime," and the people who tend to dominate the discussion will be balanced out. A circle of four doesn't need an experienced leader, and it's a great way to identify and train a coleader.

Question 3. Remember that your group may become boring if you let every group member answer a question like this one or questions 4–6. Two or three responses are plenty. The sheep pen is the place where the sheep are safe. Jesus is like the gate in that the only way to get into the safe place is through him. The safe place—the place of salvation—is the kingdom of God, the realm where everyone fulfills God's purposes and where life is therefore rich and full.

Also remember that if people are silent before they answer, it's because they're thinking!

Questions 4 and 5. Jesus calls each of us by name. He leads us. He makes sure we get the nourishment we need. He protects us from evil (wolves), even at the cost of his life. Whenever we doubt that he has our best interests at heart, his willingness to die for us is the answer to our fears.

Questions 6, 8, 9, and 10. These questions are designed to let group members voice not just their joyful experiences of Jesus' care, but also their confusion and pain. You may have a seeker or new believer who hasn't yet experienced Jesus as Shepherd but who has experienced plenty of wolves. You may have a longtime believer who has suffered and wonders why his or her life doesn't seem abundant or well cared for. These people need you to be the Good Shepherd's hands, eyes, and ears in this conversation. They need you to be sensitive and care about their pain. You don't need to solve their problems. You don't need to defend God or answer their questions and doubts. You just need to listen and care.

There are no quick fixes to complex problems. Minimizing someone's pain by trying to solve it quickly prevents you from communicating a shepherd's heart. God is very capable of healing someone's hurts. Try to avoid covering your awkwardness in the moment by filling it with words.

You may decide that someone's need is so important that the group should stop for a while and care for her. Or, you may decide after a few minutes to put a hand on someone's shoulder, pray briefly and compassionately for him, and let the group move on. It's okay if someone cries—just pass the tissues. Model Paul's teaching that we are to mourn with those who mourn (Romans 12:15). You can see why this would be a good time to gather in smaller (safer) circles for this discussion.

Abundant life, or life to the full, isn't the absence of pain here and now. Nearly all the apostles suffered terribly, and many were tortured and killed, but their lives were full because they had the moment-by-moment awareness of the Shepherd feeding their souls. Your group members don't need you to lecture them about this. They need you to demonstrate it by the way you deal with your own suffering, by your eagerness to spend personal time with God, and by the way you care for them when they're in pain.

Questions 12 and 13. As leader, you're in the people development business. Part of your job is to help others discover and develop their gifts. You may not need their help to plan a party or lead a meeting, but they need you to let them take on a role and support them so that they succeed. If you have children, you know that it's often easier to do a job yourself than to help someone else learn to do it. But that's what Jesus did with his disciples, and it's what he wants us to do for those we lead.

SESSION FOUR:
THE SERVANT

The Bible is clear that every Christian is meant to be a servant of Christ. We strongly recommend you challenge your members to take whatever step that they sense God is calling them to and that will challenge them. You will need to model here. Don't miss the need people have to grow through sharing responsibilities to host the group.

Question 1. You may want to affirm someone who is or has been a servant in your group—maybe behind the scenes—and then ask the group to do the same for others.

Question 3. Make sure everyone understands what foot washing signified in that ancient culture. It's important to strip the glamour off servanthood. You may want to select some Study Notes to read together. Serving can be dirty and thankless, like caring for small children with messy diapers. Jesus had no self-focused motives for doing it. He did it because he loved his disciples and because he wanted them to learn to love each other in the same way.

If you really want to bring home this message to your group, wash some people's feet as they arrive or during the meeting. If you're worried about people saying no, wash your spouse's or coleader's feet. This will create a memory that you and your group will never forget. One group did this and still describes the evening as one of the most memorable in their group's ten-year history. Have a chair, warm water, soft music, and a stack of towels ready.

Question 4. Genuine love will always produce service. To love is to will the other's good, and that always leads to loving actions.

Also, service should always be an expression of love. Among the people of God, no one should be forced to serve or be manipulated into serving. Those who serve because they fear those they serve, or because of guilt or manipulation, need the church's support in addressing those situations. The most loving thing the community can do for those who demand service, or who manipulate others, is to confront them about this behavior. Jesus was fearless and not subject to manipulation, so he could serve out of love.

Questions 5, 6, and 7. Jesus knew that he had come from God and was going to God, and that his status with the Father was so secure that earthly humiliation couldn't threaten it. Those who let themselves be walked on tend to be motivated by fear, guilt, or shame. Manipulators use our fear or shame to control us. When we know what Jesus knew, we can't be controlled by fear or shame, so we're free to do whatever we believe is the most loving thing in the situation. Sometimes that means serving others beyond what they ask for (Matthew 5:38–42). Sometimes it means standing up to them, even if (as happened to Jesus) we will suffer for doing so.

Question 8. Peter didn't think someone with higher status should serve someone with lower status in such a menial way. His attitude was partly humble and accurate, but it was shot through with threads of pride. After all, when he was a master in Jesus' kingdom, he didn't intend to do menial things for his subordinates! Jesus had to shake him out of that ego-driven attitude. The kingdom of God is a realm where greatness is measured by our willingness to get down and dirty for others.

Question 10. This question is key. For some people, just exerting themselves enough to share in providing refreshments for the group or cleaning up after meetings would be a step forward. Some need to learn the kind of listening that is deeply healing to the speaker. Others do these kinds of service as a matter of course (along with changing diapers and cleaning bathrooms). You may want to call attention to those group members who have been serving your group in various ways during the past four meetings.

If you as leader have been doing all the serving in your group, this is the time to give others a chance. Ask for a volunteer to handle the group's Prayer and Praise Report, and check in with those who have asked for prayer. Let people know they could plan worship for the group.

Question 12. People need to go beyond theorizing about service to actually doing it. Try to come to this question prepared to get the discussion started with your own personal examples and ideas. Also, ask your pastor if there are any needs in the congregation that your group could fill: an elderly person who could use a Saturday morning yard cleanup, or someone just out of the hospital who is not yet able to clean her house. Be sure to check out the website at www.lifetogether.com for twenty-five group serving ideas.

Encourage your group to see the world through Jesus' eyes. Looking though the eyes of a servant is not easy, but it is one of the most powerful principles in the Christian life. Cast the vision to the group and assign two people to plan your group's serving project. Some leaders have the members select who will plan the event.

Question 13. The secret servant exercise will only take a minute and will really warm up the group. Have the paper and pens ready to go. Make sure every member is covered, especially those who are absent.

One final thing in this session is to confirm the group's interest in continuing to another study in this series. Show them the next study guide and collect the money in advance, or pick up the books and have them pay you later.

SESSION FIVE:
THE SAVIOR

Question 3. This session departs from your usual Bible study format. Instead of taking a passage apart verse by verse, you're going to put yourselves into the passage. The emphasis is on *heart* learning over *head* learning. If you wish, the For Deeper Study questions will take you into Paul's letters to see how he explained the cross. But the core passage in John looks at the story rather than the explanation. It's important to grasp that we are part of the story. It wasn't the Jews or the Romans who killed Christ. We did it. We wanted God dead so we could run the world our way. He willingly died in our place.

If you think you might not get volunteers easily, you may want to take people aside before the meeting starts and ask them to read certain parts. Let people say no if they choose—some people aren't comfortable reading aloud. Be sure everyone understands that *everyone*—even those who have other roles—will read the words of the Crowd.

Consider having some highlighters available so people can mark their parts.

Questions 5–11. Select among these questions to the degree you have time. Groups doing deeper Bible study will want to spend more time with these questions. Others may want to choose one or two questions to discuss.

Question 12. The penalty for every sin you have ever committed, even those in your future, has been paid for.

Question 13. An outward focus can be a turning point in the health of your group. You are the number-one factor in making it happen. We urge you to give serious consideration to this item. We've worked with churches where group members took time out to launch new groups, and the results have been terrific. The old groups didn't fall apart; in fact, they were revitalized when members came back fired up by their experience of leadership. The boost in personal growth is huge. If you have just one couple willing to take this risk, give them every encouragement. Plan to pray for them and release them in session 6.

Ideally, you can pass leadership of your current group to someone else while you take a break to launch a new group. This will show the group you mean business about playing your part in fulfilling the Great Commission. The adventure begins here!

Question 16. Some churches permit groups to celebrate Communion within their group. If yours does, this would be a great way to end this meeting or your next meeting. Otherwise, your group can attend a worship service together sometime when the Lord's Supper will be shared, and you can make this a group experience.

Question 17. Play one of the quieter worship songs from the LIFE TOGETHER CD (or a CD of your choice), letting everyone listen and reflect on what Jesus did on the cross. *Do not* put pressure on anyone to accept Christ. As the song ends, you can begin to pray for the requests that were shared in question 15, or you can play the song again and softly sing to the Father as a prayer.

If you have seekers in your group, chat with them after the meeting to see how the group is going for them. Don't send any subtle messages about trusting Christ. Give them complete freedom to be as open or reserved as they want about their process.

Explore with your pastor or church staff the possibility of baptism for any new believers. Be sure to be part of the celebration when it happens.

SESSION SIX:
THE RISEN LORD

Whether your group is ending or continuing, it's important to celebrate where you have come together. If you choose not to discuss question 1 during your meeting, this would be a great question to discuss at a party. Be sure the spiritual partner time is honored.

Thank everyone for what they've contributed to the group. You might even give some thought ahead of time to something unique each person has contributed. You can say those things at the beginning of your meeting.

Most of the Bible study questions in this session aim to help your group understand what actually happened that first Easter. The Gospels record the facts of the resurrection. Question 9 invites you to discuss how the rest of the New Testament explores the implications of this event. Unless your group is looking up the passages as homework, you probably won't have time to discuss each item in question 9 in detail. You might choose one implication from that list for the group to discuss.

Question 3. Peter heard Mary exclaim that Jesus' body has been stolen. The passage doesn't say what he or the other disciples said, or what Peter may have heard from John in the empty tomb. Peter saw Mary in the predawn darkness. We don't know how much light there was by the time Peter and John reached the tomb. But the key things he sees are the open tomb (not closed by a stone as it had been) and the burial cloths. Thieves were unlikely to have unwrapped the body.

Question 4. It's possible that it was still too dark for her to see Jesus clearly, or that the sun was in her eyes and his face was in shadow, or that her tears blinded her. It's also possible that in his resurrected state, Jesus looked somewhat different from the way he looked when Mary last saw him. Healthier? Younger? Entirely different? We don't know.

Question 5. Jesus had become someone Mary had never known—a person raised from death. He was about to be glorified to the Father's side, as he had been for eternity past. Yet despite this huge gulf between Jesus and Mary, his death and resurrection had made it possible to say that his relationship to God—my Father, my God—was now equally intimate for her.

Question 7. In his resurrection appearances, Jesus seems to have made a point of doing things that showed he was not a ghost or disembodied spirit.

Mary apparently could cling to him (John 20:17); he had wounds that could be touched (John 20:27); he ate food (Luke 24:37–43). At that time, most Jews believed they would be resurrected bodily at the end of the age. But Greeks believed that after death, souls would live forever in a disembodied state. This Greek belief spread widely through the Roman world and remains common today, even among Christians. If the continued life of his soul was all that happened to Jesus, then it would not have been considered remarkable then or now. What shocked people about the disciples' claim was that they said they had seen Jesus *with a body*. Greeks viewed bodies as the source of most human ills; many people looked forward to shedding their bodies at death. But the Christian (and traditional Jewish) claim is that we will have bodies—better ones—for eternity.

Question 8. Jesus gave his followers a supernatural peace and well-being that no suffering in this life could destroy. That was good, because he also laid his own mission on their shoulders, and this was bound to lead to all sorts of suffering. The main goal of some religions is to give people inner peace. Christian faith is not one of those religions. The mission of drawing all creation into God's kingdom is primary, and peace is one of the more pleasant by-products of accepting that mission.

Question 9. You could spend a whole meeting just studying each of the ideas in this list. But if your time is limited, choose one of the implications for the group to focus on. Which one do you think they most need to understand? It will be helpful if you read the Bible passages ahead of time.

ABOUT THE AUTHORS

The authors' previous work as a team includes the DOING LIFE TOGETHER Bible study series, which won a Silver Medallion from the Evangelical Christian Publishers Association, as well as the DOING LIFE TOGETHER DVD series.

Brett Eastman has served as the champion of Small Groups and Leadership Development for both Willow Creek Community Church and Saddleback Valley Community Church. Brett is now the Founder and CEO of Lifetogether, a ministry whose mission is to "transform lives through community." Brett earned his Masters of Divinity degree from Talbot School of Theology and his Management Certificate from Kellogg School of Business at Northwestern University. **Dee Eastman** is the real hero in the family, who, after giving birth to Joshua and Breanna, gave birth to identical triplets— Meagan, Melody, and Michelle. They live in Las Flores, California.

Todd and Denise Wendorff serve at King's Harbor Church in Redondo Beach, California. Todd is a teaching pastor, handles leadership development, and pastors men. He is also coauthor of the Every Man Bible Study Series. Denise speaks to women at conferences, classes, and special events. She also serves women through personal discipleship. Previously, Todd was on the pastoral staff at Harvest Bible Chapel, Willow Creek Community Church, and Saddleback Valley Community Church. He holds a Th.M. from Talbot School of Theology. Todd and Denise live in Rolling Hills Estates, California with their three children, Brooke, Brittany, and Brandon.

Karen Lee-Thorp has written or cowritten more than fifty books and Bible studies, including *How to Ask Great Questions* and *Why Beauty Matters.* Her previous Silver Medallion winners are *The Story of Stories, LifeChange: Ephesians,* and *LifeChange: Revelation.* She was a senior editor at NavPress for many years and series editor for the LifeChange Bible study series. She is now a freelance writer, speaks at women's retreats, and trains small group leaders. She lives in Brea, California, with her husband, Greg Herr, and their daughters, Megan and Marissa.

SMALL GROUP ROSTER

Name	Address	Phone	Email Address	Team or Role	Church Ministry
Bill Jones	7 Alvalar Street L.F. 92665	766-2255	bjones@aol.com	socials	children's ministry

(Pass your book around your group at your first meeting to get everyone's name and contact information.)

Name	Address	Phone	Email Address	Team or Role	Church Ministry

Experiencing Christ Together:
Living with Purpose in Community
Brett & Dee Eastman; Todd & Denise Wendorff;
Karen Lee-Thorp

Experiencing Christ Together: Living with Purpose in Community is a series of six, six-week study guides that offers small groups a chance to explore Jesus' teaching on the five biblical purposes of the church. By closely examining Christ's life and teaching in the Gospels, the series helps group members walk in the steps of Christ's early followers. Jesus lived every moment following God's purposes for his life, and Experiencing Christ Together helps groups learn how they can do this too. The first book lays the foundation: who Christ is and what he has done for us. Each of the other five books in the series looks at how Jesus trained his followers to live one of the five biblical purposes (fellowship, discipleship, service, evangelism, and worship).

	Softcovers	DVD
Beginning in Christ Together	ISBN: 0-310-24986-4	ISBN: 0-310-26187-2
Connecting in Christ Together	ISBN: 0-310-24981-3	ISBN: 0-310-26189-9
Growing in Christ Together	ISBN: 0-310-24985-6	ISBN: 0-310-26192-9
Serving Like Christ Together	ISBN: 0-310-24984-8	ISBN: 0-310-26194-5
Sharing Christ Together	ISBN: 0-310-24983-X	ISBN: 0-310-26196-1
Surrendering to Christ Together	ISBN: 0-310-24982-1	ISBN: 0-310-26198-8

Pick up a copy today at your favorite bookstore!

ZONDERVAN™

GRAND RAPIDS, MICHIGAN 49530 USA

WWW.ZONDERVAN.COM

life**together**.com

Doing Life Together series

Brett & Dee Eastman; Todd & Denise Wendorff;
Karen Lee-Thorp

Based on the five biblical purposes that form the bedrock of Saddleback Church, Doing Life Together will help your group discover what God created you for and how you can turn this dream into an everyday reality. Experience the transformation firsthand as you begin Connecting, Growing, Developing, Sharing, and Surrendering your life together for him.

"Doing Life Together is a groundbreaking study ... [It's] the first small group curriculum built completely on the purpose-driven paradigm ... The greatest reason I'm excited about [it] is that I've seen the dramatic changes it produces in the lives of those who study it."

—FROM THE FOREWORD BY RICK WARREN

Small Group Ministry Consultation

Building a healthy, vibrant, and growing small group ministry is challenging. That's why Brett Eastman and a team of certified coaches are offering small group ministry consultation. Join pastors and church leaders from around the country to discover new ways to launch and lead a healthy Purpose-Driven small group ministry in your church. To find out more information please call 1-800-467-1977.

	Softcover	
Beginning Life Together	ISBN: 0-310-24672-5	ISBN: 0-310-25004-8
Connecting with God's Family	ISBN: 0-310-24673-3	ISBN: 0-310-25005-6
Growing to Be Like Christ	ISBN: 0-310-24674-1	ISBN: 0-310-25006-4
Developing Your SHAPE to Serve Others	ISBN: 0-310-24675-X	ISBN: 0-310-25007-2
Sharing Your Life Mission Every Day	ISBN: 0-310-24676-8	ISBN: 0-310-25008-0
Surrendering Your Life for God's Pleasure	ISBN: 0-310-24677-6	ISBN: 0-310-25009-9
Curriculum Kit	ISBN: 0-310-25002-1	

ZONDERVAN™

GRAND RAPIDS, MICHIGAN 49530 USA

WWW.ZONDERVAN.COM

lifetogether.com